EASTON AREA PUBLIC LIB.

1901 9100 036 358 7

D0811883

NO LONGER PROPERTY
OF EASTON AREA
PUBLIC LIBRARY

LEISURE AND PLEASURE
IN THE NINETEENTH CENTURY

By the same author
JOURNEY BY STAGES

The Prince Regent at Brighton
by Robert Cruikshank

LEISURE AND PLEASURE IN THE NINETEENTH CENTURY

BY

Stella Margetson

COWARD-McCANN, Inc.
NEW YORK

EASTON PUBLIC LIBRARY
EASTON PA

914.2
M328p

First American Edition 1969
Copyright © 1969 by Stella Margetson

*All rights reserved. This book, or parts thereof, may not be repro-
duced in any form without permission in writing from the Publisher.*

Library of Congress Catalog Card Number: 75–75749

PRINTED IN THE UNITED STATES OF AMERICA

JUN 18 1969

EASTON PUBLIC LIBRARY
EASTON PA

With love to dear Margaret and Johnnie

ACKNOWLEDGEMENTS

I would like to acknowledge my great debt to the authors and editors of the works listed in the Bibliography at the end of this book.

To pick and choose a path through the voluminous literature of and about the nineteenth century is a formidable task, and to acknowledge each author separately an impossibility. But I would like to thank all those and their publishers who have allowed me to quote from the original diaries, journals and letters written within the period, and all those who have helped me to understand the people of the Regency and the Victorian Age.

I would also like to thank the librarians and staff of the British Museum, the Guildhall Library, the Victoria and Albert Museum, the Westminster Public Libraries and the Fawcett Library for their kindness and their patience.

CONTENTS

LIST OF ILLUSTRATIONS

Frontispiece

THE PRINCE REGENT AT BRIGHTON by Robert
Cruikshank
Victoria and Albert Museum

Between pages 36 and 37

ASTLEY'S ROYAL AMPHITHEATRE by Pugin and
Rowlandson, 1808
Mansell Collection

CREMORNE PLEASURE GARDENS
Radio Times Hulton Picture Library

RAMSGATE SANDS by W. P. Frith, RA, 1854
Radio Times Hulton Picture Library

ALMACK's by I. R. and G. Cruikshank, 1821
Mansell Collection

COUNT D'ORSAY AT CROCKFORD'S, 1843
Mansell Collection

Between pages 180 and 181

QUEEN VICTORIA AND PRINCE ALBERT IN SCOTLAND
by Sir Edwin Landseer, RA, 1852
Radio Times Hulton Picture Library

A TRIP TO GREENWICH ON EASTER MONDAY, 1847
Mansell Collection

LEISURE AND PLEASURE
IN THE NINETEENTH CENTURY

1

THE
PRINCE
REGENT

IT IS ONLY in our time that leisure and pleasure have become a subject for analysis. In the nineteenth century leisure was no problem to the people who enjoyed it and pleasure was not identified with mechanical entertainment—it depended on the individual, on his social background and his singularity of taste. One man's meat was another's poison.

Leisure among the upper classes was a rule of life; no gentleman ever boasted of doing anything, no lady ever wanted to be caught doing what could be done for her. And taking pleasure in its widest sense as any form of satisfaction or delight experienced by men and women in the course of their personal lives, no century was more rich in variety, more infinite in its contrasts or more confident. The English believed there was no one in the world like them. They believed in themselves and their own superiority. They were not haunted by fear of the future nor unduly ashamed of the past. They enjoyed their own way of life, whether in the self-indulgent days of the Regency, in the more sober world of Victorian gentility or in the Bohemian explosion of the nineties. And there was room for expansion, for the development of character and personality; time to stand and stare and to gratify every idiosyncrasy of the human heart and mind.

Indeed, England at the beginning of the century was a paradise for any gentleman intent upon leading a life of pleasure. London was the most opulent and the gayest capital in the world, Brighton the playground of Europe. The great mansions of the nobility, set in their green parklands and groves of mature trees, and the smaller houses staffed by a horde of servants indoors and out, gave their owners leisure enough to enjoy all the delights of the country. There was hunting, shooting and fishing; prize-fighting, horse-racing and gambling. And a lord was expected to behave like a lord: the more eccentric the better, for then he carried the populace with him and gave them a chance to share his fun, or, in London, afforded the rabble endless amusement by the figure he cut and the money he spent on his own entertainment. He had nothing to worry him except his debts and they were a symptom suffered by most of his friends in the giddy world that revolved round His Royal Highness the Prince of Wales.

The Prince—not formally designated Regent until 1811 —was the undisputed leader of high society. To catch his eye as Beau Brummell did, to please him or amuse him was enough to ensure a successful career in the *beau monde*; to upset him and bring on one of his tantrums led to the instant, cutting withdrawal of his friendship—a serious hazard as he grew older and his temper became more uncertain. By 1800 he was not yet forty, but his shapely legs were thickening and his habit of sitting up late and drinking cherry brandy in the overheated splendour of

Carlton House or the Pavilion at Brighton had begun to diminish his charm as well as to increase his waistline. The time would come when the stiffest corset could not conceal nor control the swelling body in its tight 'unmentionables,' the Regency 'trowsers' he and the dandies had made *de rigueur*, a time when the cartoonists would be quick to make painful fun of his infirmities and he could no longer bear to be seen; but that time was not yet. He still had an enormous zest for pleasure, for riding and driving, for music and dancing and amorous adventure, and was still bent on carrying the uninhibited gusto of his youth into the dissipations of middle age. Given his hereditary background—the Hanoverian mixture of coarseness, insanity and stupidity—and his oppressive upbringing, it is greatly to his credit that he ever developed at all into the elegant creature described as the First Gentleman in Europe and, by the Duke of Wellington, who never sought to flatter anyone dead or alive, as 'the most extraordinary compound of talent, wit, buffoonery, obstinacy and good-feeling—in short a medley of the most opposite qualities with a great preponderance of good that I ever saw in any character in my life.'

Opposite qualities in the Prince's character certainly bedevilled his behaviour. He could be riotous, vulgar, obscene, yet as sensitive as a woman, as fond as a child and often, at his most unexpected, humanly kind to ordinary people. He was never the useless, unthinking, drunken rake his enemies believed him to be, but a man whose vanity was bound to become inflated as he made his way through the treacherous air of sycophancy his position at first commanded. A more sober mind might well have floundered, a steadier spirit have been confounded, for as well as his wits, he needed buffoonery, guts and gaiety to survive the extravagant age he brought to fruition.

Moreover, talent in the Prince was combined with taste and aesthetic feeling, sometimes gaudy, fanciful and extreme, but always original. From the age of twenty-one when he first broke away from the stifling Court of his father, King George III, to the day of his death forty-seven years later, his pleasure in the arts never wearied. He had a genuine, passionate love of beauty, which found its expression in a thousand different ways: from the cut of a coat to the exquisite design of a jewelled snuff-box, from the flamboyant attire of his favourite Hussars to the silken foot of his latest mistress, and, above all, through the architects he employed on his grandiose building schemes. Henry Holland, James Wyatt, John Nash and Decimus Burton were men who respected the creative ideas of their royal master and found his frank enjoyment of their work stimulating, even when they had to wait a long time to get paid for it. They were his allies against the philistine House of Commons, forever trying to curb his expenditure, the critics who carped and the people who frowned on his flights of fancy.

Carlton House with its porphyry columns, glittering chandeliers and velvet carpets, and its superb vista on the ground floor through the double doors of the Library, the Golden Drawing-Room and the Gothic Dining-Room into the Conservatory, rivalled the Palace of Versailles in its day of glory. Some of the ladies and gentlemen of high rank and fashion who attended the routs there, complained that the rooms outshone their most spectacular jewellery and the clothes they wore, reflecting from one giant mirror to another the kaleidoscopic patterns of their gold-encrusted ornamentation. Yet the Pavilion at Brighton, with its exuberant facade and its voluptuous interior of fabulous Indo-Chinese decoration, was even more fantastic and wonderful. And this was the Prince's own romantic conception, his 'stately pleasure-dome' beside the sea, if, in the opinion of some, it was also his most extravagant folly. The money he spent did not concern him; he could not stop, he had to go on. The sinuous design of a scarlet dragon in Chinese lacquer or the delicate, detailed tracery of a tented ceiling so excited his fertile imagination that he could not be happy until he had found some means of turning his vaulting ideas into fact—and then the result did not always satisfy, for what was reality compared with the vision of a man so greedy for aesthetic pleasure?

With John Nash at his elbow he saw the vision of a new London, more elegant and beautiful than anything anyone had ever thought of, in the maze of tumbledown streets between Soho and the Georgian squares of Mayfair—the vision of a stately avenue from Carlton House all the way to the old Royal Park of Marylebone. Money was difficult—it always was when the Regent had a plan; and the long war with France, in spite of Nelson's triumph at Trafalgar and Wellington's foothold in the Peninsula, had not yet turned to victory when the scheme was first outlined. But Nash and the Prince fought their own battles against the fiercest opposition, and by 1822 the new Regent Street with its handsome colonnades, its curving Quadrant and long vista to the church in Langham Place had given London a superb new thoroughfare at a cost of nearly a million pounds. Then came the Regent's Canal and the work through which Nash and the Prince will ever be remembered—Regent's Park, with its lyrical scenery, elegant villas and gleaming terraces, a townscape that has never been surpassed or equalled.

Much criticism was thrown at Nash for using stucco instead of stone, much fury levelled at his head for debauching the taste of the Regent and building with tawdry, insubstantial materials in a pseudo-classical style. Maria Edgeworth, on a visit to London in 1830, though 'properly surprised by the new town that has been built in the Regent's Park', was indignant 'at plaister statues and horrid useless *domes* and pediments crowded with mock sculpture figures which damp and smoke must destroy in a season or two', adding 'there is ever some voice which cries Must fall! Must fall! Must scale off—soon, soon, soon!' But Crabb Robinson, writing some years later with more perception, declared: 'I really think this enclosure, with the new street leading to it from Carlton House, will give a sort of glory to the Regent's Government, which will be more felt by remote posterity than the victories of Trafalgar and Waterloo.'

Meanwhile, the Regent, to please himself and the populace as well, had employed Nash to design the victory celebrations in 1814, believing in common with everyone else that Napoleon was humbly eating the bread of repentance on the Island of Elba. Nothing on such a scale had ever been organized before and the preparations took so long, the event could not take place until August, by which time rejoicings for the victorious peace were becoming a little stale and it was decided to celebrate the centenary of the Hanoverian accession to the throne instead. The Royal Parks were thrown open to the public, with gambling and drinking booths in Hyde Park and a mock naval battle on the Serpentine; a sham Castle of Discord in the Green Park, timed to explode at midnight to reveal a revolving Temple of Peace hopefully attended by a choir of Vestal Virgins in transparent draperies—the Regent's own idea, this; and a seven-storeyed Chinese pagoda on the bridge over the canal in St James's Park, which did explode accidentally in the midst of the firework display, killing one spectator, though everyone else thought its column of fire was an intended part of the fun.

The Regent had personally selected the Roman Candles, Girandoles, Jerbs and Gillockes in brilliant fire, and Charles Lamb, standing in the crowd, thought the rockets 'in clusters, in trees and all shapes, spreading about like young stars in the making' were splendid. But the aftermath was not so pleasant. 'All that was countrify'd in the Parks is all but obliterated', Lamb continued in a letter to Wordsworth. 'The very colour of the green is vanished, the whole surface of Hyde Park is dry crumbling sand (*Arabia Arenosa*), not a vestige or hint of grass ever having grown there; booths and drinking places go all around it for a mile and a half . . . the stench in liquors, bad tobacco, dirty people and provisions, conquers the air, and we are stifled and suffocated.' And indeed, long after the celebrations were over and respectable people had gone home to bed, the riff-raff stayed in the gambling booths, drinking and swearing—and were still there a week later when the Home Secretary, Lord Sidmouth, had to intervene to extinguish their rowdy behaviour.

Unhappily none of all this made the Regent any more popular with the mob or with his more sober-minded critics. It was only at Brighton, in the glittering new bow-windowed town beside the sea which he had made so fashionable, that he could relax and indulge in the passion for horses he shared with the nation. Here, his skill was freely admired, whether in driving his phaeton at a pace along the crowded Steyne or riding out to review his brilliantly accoutred Hussars on the green slope of the downs. And at the races, guarded by Johnny Townsend, who kept his royal master's purse for him as well as undesirable people at a distance from him, he was in his element and at his ease with his sporting friends, Sir John Lade, the Earl of Jersey, the Duke of Bedford, Sir John Shelley and others. Later the whole party would return to the Pavilion for a sumptuous banquet with dish after dish piled high with tasty con-coctions of fish, meat and poultry and sweets bubbling over with chocolate and cream, and while the bottles

circulated round the table and his German band played
in the ante-room, the Prince beat time on a dinner gong.
What man devoted to pleasure could ask for more? Yet
there were some disgruntled guests like Creevey, the
Member of Parliament for Thetford, who found the
heavy drinking and the heavy eating, the loud music and
the heat a bit of a bore, though even he had to admit that
the Prince 'behaved with the greatest good humour . . .
was always merry and full of his jokes, and anyone would
have said he was really a happy man.'

Perhaps he was—at the beginning when Mrs Fitzherbert
held his heart. She was plump and pretty with golden
hair and an English rose complexion; twice a widow but
still in her twenties when the Prince first met her, and a
woman of the utmost discretion. Unlike Lady Jersey
and Lady Hertford, who supplanted her in the Prince's
affections, she had no political axe to grind and much
preferred a quiet life to one exposed to the public eye. It
was her misfortune—and the Prince's—that his lust for
pleasure was so violent, it pitched him headlong into the
arms of the other two ladies. He was easily infatuated,
emotionally unstable and ready to weep copious tears or
to threaten suicide if he could not at once get his way.

Yet it is doubtful whether he really got much pleasure
from either of his new adventures. The ambitious
Countess of Jersey deliberately set out to snare him when
he was still young enough to be foolish and, not content
with his princely adoration, there was nothing she did
not do to make his marriage with the Princess Caroline
even more distasteful to him than it was. She put Epsom
salts in Caroline's soup on the wedding night, intercepted
that unhappy and eccentric lady's intimate correspondence with her mother and pinpricked the Prince with her
own mischievous tongue. For two or three years when
his passion began to cool, he went in terror of the
scheming Countess and at last when he broke away, he

gladly returned like a child with a raging fever to the bosom of Mrs Fitzherbert. 'If she is as *true* as I think she is *wise*,' Mrs Creevey wrote to her husband, 'she is an extraordinary person, and most worthy to be beloved'— and so, for a time, it seemed. The Prince and Mrs Fitzherbert were happy together and her influence on him was wholly good. 'My neighbours here go on most lovingly,' wrote Sir Harry Englefield from Brighton, adding with a malicious delight: 'Their affection seems to grow with their growth and fatten with their fat.' Sir Harry, however, had not reckoned with Lady Hertford, and neither had Mrs Fitzherbert. Her truth and her wisdom never faltered in the testing time ahead; it was the Prince who lied and behaved like a cad, showing his worst and most brutal side in his manner of dismissing her to make the way clear for the pursuit of his new pleasure.

What the Regent saw in the high Tory, haughty and frigid dame of the Marquis of Hertford, already past her prime in looks and magnetism, it is difficult to imagine. Perhaps it was the attraction of opposites, a craving to be admired by someone—outwardly at least—so respectable; an attempt on the Regent's part to put away the follies of his youth and to veneer them with a dignity more suitable to his new status. He was at all events a spaniel at her feet and apparently quite unaware that her family and her friends were collecting political appointments by the dozen owing to his inability to make a decision without her approval. Almost every day in the afternoon in London, he was driven in his yellow chariot to Hertford House in Manchester Square with his superb bay horses prancing ahead and the purple blinds drawn, there to be received by the Marquis, who tactfully bowed himself backwards out of the drawing-room as soon as his royal visitor had settled on a couch by his connubial lady. No amount of ridicule and no hostility from his former friends among the Whigs had the slightest effect on the Regent. Quite besotted and befuddled by the lady's charms, he went his way with sublime indifference until his old mad father died and at last he was King; then to the astonishment of everyone, with the crown upon his head and the sceptre in his hand, he fell out of love with Lady Hertford and into love with Lady Conyngham.

By then he was fifty-eight and his indiscretions were catching up with him. He suffered from gout and dropsy, shortness of breath and fits of depression, and his temper had not improved. But the Marchioness, herself a full-blown, opulent flower of over fifty, whose fair hair and pink complexion perhaps reminded him of his darling Fitzherbert, made life more pleasant for him at a time when his legitimate Queen was behaving like a virago and his unpopularity with the nation had reached a terrifying pitch of hysterical violence. Lady Conyngham did not bully him and seldom bored him; and if she was sometimes bored herself by the way he sat kissing her hand or 'pouted and sulked' unless she followed him from one room to another, she did not show it; after all, he gave her some splendid diamonds and a sapphire which some people said belonged to the crown jewels, and her husband and her sons were appointed to high office in the Royal Household, while her daughter acted as her chaperon.

The King did not hear—or pretended not to—the acid comments of Lady Hertford. He took the Conyngham family to Brighton, where at last the Pavilion was finished, with pipes laid from the sea to his private bathroom so that he could enjoy splashing about in his own sea water in the hope of being invigorated. The rooms were as hot as ever and the food as rich—he could never resist the syllabubs with cream or the meringues piled high with sugar; and he still enjoyed his musical evenings, on one occasion entertaining Signor

Rossini, the glamorous young composer from Italy, and
Michael Kelly, the Irish singer, who was old now but
remembered Mozart. And yet there was something
indefinable—a shadow here, a skeleton there, vague and
uncomfortable. Could it be that the pleasure dome was
losing its savour, that pleasure itself was beginning to
pall as the payment for it mounted up in physical pain
and mental neurosis?

Suddenly, when the people of Brighton wrote something rude about their royal master and his new favourite,
the King left in a terrible huff for Windsor, there to give
way to his morbid fear of being seen in public and to hide
his bloated figure in the privacy of the Park and the
Castle. Lady Conyngham, to her credit, did not desert
him. She may have enjoyed the power she had over the
reigning monarch and the pleasure of being consulted
by the Duke of Wellington, and she may have been
avaricious, but she did not deserve the vicious and
libellous things that were said about her. She bore with
considerable patience the difficult moods of the King and
strove to give him sympathy at a time when the hideous,
brutal cartoons in the Press were enough to drive even a
less sensitive man out of his mind. Besides she did not
attempt to interfere with his one remaining pleasure, for
now he had finished with Brighton, he was busy with his
plans for Buckingham House and determined to improve
Windsor. He found the Castle inconvenient, a decaying,
derelict bundle of stone that had been neglected for more
than a hundred years, but he saw the grandeur and the
beauty of it and together with his chosen architect, Sir
Jeffry Wyatville, transformed it into one of the most
stately and picturesque of all the royal palaces in Europe.

This was his monument, his claim on posterity, as well
as his final achievement. Only a prince of consummate
taste and fine perceptions could have put his own personal pleasure to such a purpose, and only a prince with

passionate feeling could have written to Wellington, in defence of his architects, words that still bite with a royal fury. 'Mr Nash has been most infamously used,' he declared, when the Duke refused to grant any further money for the improvements to Buckingham House. 'If those who go through the furnace for me and for my service are not protected, the favour of the Sovereign becomes worse than nugatory'—a point that even Wellington had to admit, for whatever faults George IV had as Regent and King, stinginess to those who served him was not among them, and as a patron of the arts there were few men to equal him in generosity.

2

AN
EXCLUSIVE
WORLD

THE PRINCE'S CAPACITY for spending money was shared by the whole of society. The great aristocratic families who inherited the accumulated wealth of the eighteenth century did their best to squander the lot in the pleasure-loving days of the Regency. Gambling was a mania with them. Georgiana, the beautiful Duchess of Devonshire, could not resist it. Outwardly her life at the beginning of the new century was still an endless round of entertainment, of dazzling receptions, balls and parties, where the Whig politicians predominated and the Prince was proud to give her his arm; inwardly it was darkened by the ever-increasing, astronomical figure of her debts incurred at the gaming-tables before she died in 1806. Fox, an *habitué* of Devonshire House and of Holland House, spent night after night playing for high stakes with all the bravura and the brilliance that distinguished him as an orator and a statesman, and with disastrous results. Lords Selwyn, Carlisle, Robert Spencer and other great Whigs were equally addicted to whist and faro. At White's, Boodle's and Brooks's in St James's Street, it was nothing for a gentleman to lose £30,000 or £40,000 in a single evening. Raggett, the proprietor of White's, used to sit up with the gamblers all through the night, sending his servants to bed, so that he could sweep the carpets himself in the early hours of the morning to retrieve the gold carelessly scattered on the floor.

And very few of the noble gentlemen who played with such intensity ever emerged into the street as winners—though the Duke of Portland's father-in-law, General Scott, by dining off boiled chicken, toast and water, to keep a clear head and a cool judgement over his opponents at the whist table, succeeded in winning the enormous sum of £200,000. Fuddled with wine and sick with fatigue, but as a point of honour showing no emotion whatsoever, the less successful players crept away in the morning round to the house of 'Jew' King in Clarges Street, there to mortgage their estates still more deeply for the ready cash that would enable them to return to their pleasure the next night. 'Jew' King knew more about the complicated financial affairs of the aristocracy than anyone else in England and, not surprisingly, became extremely opulent—rich enough to keep a splendid yellow carriage and to dress his handsome wife in the height of fashion, so that every day between four and seven in the evening she was to be seen driving in the Park attended by two liveried footmen and a coachman wearing a powdered wig and gloves *à l'Henri Quatre*.

'In those days,' wrote Captain Gronow thirty years later in his *Reminiscences and Recollections*, ' "pretty horse-breakers" would not have dared to show themselves in Hyde Park; nor did you see any of the lower or middle classes of London intruding themselves in regions, which, with a sort of tacit understanding, were then given up exclusively to persons of rank and fashion. The carriage company consisted of the most celebrated beauties, amongst whom were remarked the Duchesses of Rutland, Argyll, Gordon and Bedford, Ladies Cowper, Foley, Heathcote, Louisa Lambton, Hertford and Mountjoy. The most conspicuous horsemen were the Prince Regent, accompanied by Sir Benjamin Bloomfield; the Duke of York and his old friend, Warwick Lane; the Duke of Dorset on his white horse; the Marquis of Anglesea, with his lovely daughters; Lord Harrowby and the Ladies Ryder; the Earl of Sefton and the Ladies Moly-neux; and the eccentric Earl of Morton on his long tailed grey.'

Gronow, as a young officer in the Foot Guards who had fought with Wellington in the Peninsula and at Waterloo, was more than a spectator at this elegant evening parade; coming from a distinguished Welsh family and being a very personable young man, a dandy in his dress and a good dancer, he belonged to it. He was received at Almack's and was a member of the most exclusive clubs, and, except for the time he spent mounting guard at St James's Palace, his duties never interfered with his pleasure, any more than lack of funds ever disturbed his hectic enjoyment of the London season— or not until 1823 when his debts landed him in prison for a time. To make a brave appearance riding in the Park was far more important in his opinion than to show a firm balance at the bank: 'the men were mounted on such horses as England alone could then produce', they had no equal in the world. But it was, of course, an expensive amusement to be well mounted. Lord Sefton, the hump-backed millionaire, thought nothing of paying a thousand guineas at Tattersall's for a thoroughbred, and even to hire a horse from John Tilbury of Mount Street cost twelve guineas a month without its keep.

Tilbury was one of the select tradesmen in the West

End who supplied the needs of the gentry. Hoby, the bootmaker in St James's Street, was another; and it was Hoby who first drove about London in the smart black vehicle Tilbury designed and gave his name to, which soon became the favourite type of carriage among the dashing young bloods of the day. 'When I used to see Count d'Orsay driving in his tilbury some thirty years ago, I fancied that he looked like some gorgeous dragon-fly skimming through the air,' Gronow wrote admiringly —and indeed, knowing how to drive a smart carriage, whether a phaeton as high as a first floor window, a tilbury, a Stanhope or a gig, was no less essential to the man of fashion than a good seat on a horse.

Speed, with the development of Macadam's hard roads in England, had become the absolute criterion of elegance and poise, and to drive a superb equipage very fast the ambition of every young aristocrat in the kingdom. Some learnt the art of driving or 'tooling the ribbons' as it was called, from the crack stage-coachmen on the Oxford and Holyhead Roads and as semi-professionals ran superior stage-coaches of their own down to Brighton. Others joined the select coterie of the Four-in-Hand Club run by Lord Sefton, Lord Barrymore, Colonel Berkeley, Sir John Lade and the Marquis of Worcester. They assembled in George Street, Hanover Square, before driving off in style to the Windmill at Salt Hill where a princely dinner awaited them, each 'drag' and its team of horses groomed to gorgeous perfection and a sight that never failed to attract a mob of admiring onlookers. Lord Sefton drove splendid bay horses and the Marquis of Worcester a team of greys with a panache that excited general applause—and if their horses cost a fortune, what did it matter?

To practise economy was to be so out of fashion, no gentleman in his ravenous pursuit of pleasure ever considered it; and besides it would have made him the laughing-stock of his friends, hell bent on living high in spite of the bailiffs waiting at the door and the *post-obit* bills stuffed out of sight in the ormolu writing-cabinet. Lord Alvanley, when going over his financial affairs with the help of Charles Greville, actually forgot that he owed a gambling debt of £50,000 and, when inviting a friend to dinner, wrote cheerfully: 'I have no credit with either butcher or poulterer, but if you can put up with turtle or turbot, I shall be delighted to see you'—this from the *bon vivant* who had once spent £200 on a luncheon hamper from Gunter's for a boating party and had enjoyed all the year round the luxury of a fresh apricot tart on his side-table at dinner. When at last his extravagance had utterly ruined him and he was trying to live on a mere £1,250 a year, he taught his servant to come into the room and to ask what time he would like his carriage ordered; it sounded more cheerful, he thought, and looked better, even though all his friends knew he could no longer afford a carriage or any horses to drive it.

Clothes were another equally extravagant item of expenditure, and here it was not an aristocrat, but the grandson of a valet who became the *arbiter elegantarium* of society. George Brummell went to Eton, for his father, the son of Lord Monson's exceptional servant, had risen in the world through his own perseverance and could afford to send his boys to the first school in England, where the younger of the two at once distinguished himself by wearing the wings of his white cravat over the lapels of his blue uniform coat in a manner quite different from everyone else. Either at Eton or on the terrace at Windsor one Sunday afternoon, the younger Brummell attracted the attention of the Prince of Wales—his manners were already highly sophisticated. And the Prince did not forget him; as soon as the boy reached the age of sixteen, he presented him with a cornetcy in his own regiment, the 10th Hussars.

The uniform appealed to Brummell. His duties were not onerous, and since the regiment was usually stationed in London or at Brighton to be near its Colonel-in-Chief, the young cornet's opportunity of mixing in the highest society was assured. A born *arriviste*, he made the most of it, and two years later was on sufficiently intimate terms with the Prince to beg for his release from the army because he could not tolerate the prospect of going to a dreary place like Manchester when his regiment was ordered there to subdue a riot in the cotton mills. The Prince was amused—he liked originality; and Brummell was permitted to resign and to begin his career as a gentleman of leisure.

He set up house alone in Chesterfield Street on the £30,000 he had inherited from his father's estate. Women, however much they flattered him and angled for his company, did not really interest him; he was only interested in himself and in making use of his bachelor status among them to acquire the friends he needed to make a success of his new scheme of life. A superlative cook, small, intimate dinner parties of the men he wished to cultivate, elegant surroundings and no interference appealed to him more than feminine society, and to shine in the man's world he had chosen was his only purpose. He looked at his own figure and liked what he saw; then he looked at the clothes of his friends, at the gaudy silks of the Regent with his French paste buttons, his frilly shirts and his satin breeches, and raised his eyebrows in scorn. Dress should be plain, he decided, elegant, unexceptionable: neither showy nor shabby, but perfect in every detail.

So ample was his leisure, he was able to spend some five hours every morning at his toilet: first bathing in milk, eau-de-Cologne and water, then giving an hour to his hairdresser and another two hours to 'creasing down' his starched cravat until he was satisfied with the perfect shape of its folds. A friend calling on him one morning met his valet coming out of his dressing-room with a dozen or more pieces of crumpled muslin over his arm, which he described as 'our failures'; and when at last the Beau emerged at three o'clock in the afternoon in his skin-tight 'trowsers' and flawless coat, it was the impeccable balance of his 'starcher' that gave him a look of superiority over everyone else in Mayfair. He made the reputation and the fortune of Weston, his tailor in Old Bond Street, had his Hessian boots polished in the froth of champagne and the fit of his gloves ensured by employing one firm to cut the fingers and another the thumbs. In addition he boasted of possessing three hundred and sixty-five snuff-boxes, one for every day of the year according to the season.

At least one woman, whose experience of men had made her an acute judge of character, saw through him at once. Harriette Wilson, queen of the *demi-reps* in London, wrote in her *Memoirs*: 'His maxims on dress were excellent. Besides this he was neither uneducated nor deficient. He possessed also, a sort of quaint dry humour, not amounting to anything like wit; indeed he said nothing which would bear repetition; but his affected manners and little absurdities amused for the moment. Then it became the fashion to court Brummell's society, which was enough to make many seek it who cared not for it; and many more wished to be well with him, through fear, for all knew him to be cold, heartless and satirical.'

His wit, indeed, consisted in being unspeakably rude in the politest possible way, as when the Duke of Bedford asked his opinion of a new coat he was wearing, whereupon the Beau looked him up and down and remarked: 'My dear fellow—did I hear you call that *thing* a coat?' No one, he believed, was capable of reaching his own high standard of sartorial perfection; yet the more outrageous

his remarks became, the more he received the homage
of his fellow-men. His supercilious judgements were
accepted as the word of Solomon in all his wisdom, his
effrontery and his insolence enjoyed by those to whom a
nod from him as he strolled up St James's Street was a
nugget of gold to be treasured beyond price. Even when
he went too far and likened the Prince's figure to one of
his fat servants called Ben, thereupon destroying the royal
favour he had enjoyed for so long, he continued to
dominate the idle parade of fashion until his debts made
his escape to France imperative. To stand or sit with him
in the bow window of White's was the height of glory, a
privilege granted only to the select coterie or inner circle
of the Club open to the Duke of Argyll, Lords Worcester,
Alvanley, Foley and Sefton and the dandies 'Poodle'
Byng, 'Ball' Hughes and Sir Lumley Skeffington. No
ordinary member would have dared to intrude upon the
magic circle—it simply was not done; and the young
man who sought Brummell's protection when about to
enter society, had to be content with the Beau's condescension in once giving him his arm from White's to
Watier's in Piccadilly.

Watier's was originally a dining-club founded by the
Regent's chef to offset the dullness of the dinners of
boiled fowl, oyster sauce and apple tart monotonously
served at White's and Brooks's. According to Tom
Raikes, 'the dinners were so *recherchés* and so much talked
of in the town, that all the young men of fashion and
fortune became members of it; and the most luxurious
dinners were furnished at any price, as the deep play at
night rendered all charges a matter of indifference.
Macao was the constant game, and thousands passed
from one to the other with as much facility as marbles.'

Byron, in the year that he set London on fire with his
poetry and his personality, became a member there, and
ten years later when he met Lady Blessington in Genoa,

confessed to having had quite an affection for the dandies. 'The truth is, that though I gave up the business early,' he told her, 'I had a tinge of Dandyism in my minority, and probably retained enough of it to conciliate the great ones, at four-and-twenty. I had gamed and drank, and taken my degrees in most dissipations; and having no pedantry, and not being overbearing, we ran quietly together.'

But pleasure for Byron was seldom unmixed with guilt and pain. The strange puritan streak he had inherited from the Gordons gave him no peace and all his life he was tormented by a self-conscious horror of his own lameness. Though everyone in London wanted to meet him or to be seen in his company, no one amused him for very long and the more deeply he plunged into the dissipations of society, the more disenchanted he became. He was invited to the parties at Holland House where men of intellectual distinction in politics, letters and art gathered round the dinner table under the fearsome eye and scathing tongue of the indomitable Lady Holland, and he went to the breakfast parties given by the celebrated banker-poet and patron of the arts, Samuel Rogers, who entertained his guests with a caustic wit and brilliant conversation. Yet none of these diversions wholly succeeded in satisfying his passionate temperament and although he was vain enough to go to bed every night with his curls *en papillotte* and to dine off biscuits and soda water to keep his romantic figure from going to seed, he was constantly at odds with himself and society.

Women failed him, whether they were exhibitionists like Lady Caroline Lamb and Clare Clairmont, or inhibitionists like his unfortunate wife, Annabella Milbanke; and except for his friendship with Lady Melbourne, an older and a wiser woman, and his overwhelming affection for his half-sister Augusta Leigh, which brought sheer disaster on both of them, he found no real solace in feminine company. He sought comfort instead in riding and swimming, shooting, fencing and boxing, spending some of his happiest hours in the Bond Street establishment of the famous pugilist, 'Gentleman' Jackson, the admired Champion of England. Jackson wore a scarlet jacket, lace cuffs, breeches and silk stockings and was treated with great deference by the sporting gentry; and Byron made a friend of him, hanging his picture in his house in Piccadilly Terrace and roistering round the town with him to some of the lower dives in the neighbourhood of Covent Garden and the Strand.

Low company, however, was no better than high company in mitigating the ennui that beset him. Harriette Wilson, at the brilliant masquerade organized by the members of Watier's, found him sitting alone in a quiet room away from the festive throng of dancers, with 'his bright penetrating eyes staring into space'. She was immediately overcome by his beauty and, since no woman knew so well how to fetch a man on, was somewhat taken aback when he only offered her his friendship, though she declared that she would have been afraid to love him after the notorious contempt he had shown towards Caroline Lamb and professed her willingness to accept his friendship as better than nothing. With her sharp, feminine intuition she came very near to understanding his extraordinary complexity. 'Pray, dear Lord Byron,' she wrote to him some years later, 'think of me a little now and then (I don't mean as a woman, for I shall never be a woman to you) merely as *a good little fellow* who feels a warmer interest in all that happens to you and all that annoys you than anybody else in the world. Forget me when you are *happy*; but in gloomy moments, chilly miserable weather, bad razors and cold water, perhaps you'll recollect and write to me. You can easily judge by a woman's scribbling whether her heart is with it, and you *know* I love you *honestly* and dearly.'

Very few men invited by Harriette to pursue her acquaintance were able to resist, as Byron did, giving her no more than one affectionate kiss. With her sisters Fanny and Amy, and her friend Julia Johnstone, she was the starriest of the 'Fashionable Impures' or Cyprians as they were called: a courtesan of great fascination and allure, whose wit and vitality had brought her quickly to the top of her profession and had made her the most desired of all women to both the young and the old in search of amorous pleasure. 'I shall not say why and how I became, at the age of fifteen, the mistress of the Earl of Craven,' she wrote at the beginning of her *Memoirs*. 'Whether it was love, or the severity of my father, the depravity of my own heart, or the winning arts of the noble Lord, which induced me to leave my paternal roof and place myself under his protection, does not now much signify—'; and it didn't, since from that time on Harriette never regretted the fun she enjoyed as the idol of the masculine half of the *beau monde*.

Accompanied by Fanny and Julia, she drove in the Park at the fashionable hour of five in a carriage lined in pale blue satin, with an escort of hungry gentlemen trotting beside it in the hope of obtaining a winning glance or a smile from one of these 'Three Graces'; and at night they hired a box at the King's Theatre in the Haymarket in full view of the wives of the noblemen, who, later in the evening, crowded up the stairs to Amy's informal parties in York Place, where the company in the drawing-room could be numbered from the pages of Debrett and Amy herself sat coquetting with her tall Russian, Count Benckendorff. No one at the King's Theatre took very much notice of the opera or the ballet being performed; everyone was far too busy quizzing everyone else, gossiping and laughing and commenting on who was in and who was out with whom, for the opera box was the Cyprians' shop window and a room for entertainment where introductions could be made as a preliminary to greater intimacy.

Harriette in her simple, white muslin gown, with her small waist and voluptuous bosom, her tiny hands and feet and her bright auburn curls dancing in the light of the chandeliers, had nothing to fear from any of her rivals and a great number of admirers to choose from. She was not unduly mercenary—her favours could only be bought by mutual attraction; and when she was living under the protection of one of her chosen lovers, she stayed faithful to him. Once when the Duke of Wellington arrived unannounced in the middle of the night in the pouring rain on leave from the Peninsula, he found the Duke of Argyll had forestalled him and was forced to beat a wet retreat after Argyll's night-capped head had appeared at the window in the guise of an angry duenna; but normally all visitors to Harriette's house came by appointment and such embarrassments were avoided.

The handsome, romantic-looking Lord Ponsonby was her god; she adored him and was ill for months when he terminated their liaison. 'Lord, if only you could suffer for a single day the agony of mind I endured for more than two years after Ponsonby left me, because Mrs Fanny [his wife] would have it so, you would bless your stars and good fortune, blind, deaf and lame at eighty-two, so that you could sleep an hour in forgetfulness and eat a little bit of batter pudding!' she exclaimed in a letter to Byron years afterwards; and although she recovered her spirits to some extent and continued her giddy career, she was never quite the same light-hearted creature of pleasure again.

The Marquis of Worcester, before he came of age, set the noble house of Beaufort in a roar by declaring his intention of marrying her as soon as he reached his majority. Meanwhile he furnished a house at Brighton for her, called her his 'angelick wife' and would not willingly leave her in the evenings to attend the Regent's parties at the Pavilion or get up in the mornings to go on parade with his regiment. He swore he would never abandon her and would rather give up his inheritance, but Harriette was not so sure that she wanted him for ever. 'Many women, very hard pressed *par la belle nature*, intrigue because they see no prospect nor hopes of getting husbands,' she declared, 'but I, who might have smuggled myself into the Beaufort family, by merely declaring to Lord Worcester, with my finger pointed towards the North—that way leads to Harriette Wilson's bedchamber . . . scorned the idea of taking such an advantage of the passion I had inspired, in what I believed to be a generous breast, as might hereafter cause unhappiness to himself, while it would embitter the peace of his parents.'

These noble sentiments of Harriette's were never actually put to the test. Worcester's uxorious behaviour and the pleasures of Brighton were already beginning to bore her, when his family tore him out of her arms and packed him off to Spain as aide-de-camp to the Duke of Wellington. Did the Marquis and the Duke compare notes when the fires round the camp were burning low? Perhaps. . . . The Duke was a realist; he said that forty-eight hours, the limit he set for his officers' leave in Lisbon, was 'as long as any reasonable man could wish to spend in bed with any woman'. But Worcester, it seems, did not have to go as far as Lisbon to enjoy himself, for he soon found consolation in the frisky little wife of one of the Paymasters to the Forces, thereby leaving Harriette free to renew her acquaintance with Mr Meyler, who was known in London as the rich sugar baker. His affections at one time were said to be 'divided between a Mrs Bang, a Mrs Patten and a Mrs Pancrass, all ladies of Covent Garden notoriety', but Harriette's invitation enthralled him and he promptly set up house with her in the Marylebone New Road. Unhappily he proved to be one of the most ill-tempered of Harriette's lovers, capable of rousing her to such violent fits of jealousy that she often kicked him out of bed 'as soon as he became restive', though she excused him afterwards when she wrote of him: 'There was an expression in Meyler's countenance of such voluptuous beauty, that it was impossible for any woman to converse with him, after he had dined, in cold blood.'

None of the Cyprians expected conversation with a gentleman to be all he required, yet most of them were clever enough to be very entertaining; and at the ball they gave once a year in the Argyle Rooms, dressed in all their finery of plumed turbans, *décolleté* gowns and satin slippers, they abandoned themselves to a riotous orgy of pleasure. According to the description of one writer: 'While the snowy orbs of nature undisguised heaved like the ocean with circling swell, the amorous lover palmed the melting fair and led her to where shame-faced Aurora might hope in vain to draw aside the curtain and penetrate the mysteries of Cytherea'—thus bringing the evening to its desired conclusion.

Besides Harriette and her sisters and Julia Johnstone, there were other Fashionable Impures called the Mocking Bird, the Venus Mendicant, and the White Doe, who 'reclined upon the velvet cushions of Independence'; Laura who had 'money in the Funds', and Brazen Bellona, whose father had been a market gardener in Eton, conveniently close to the College for the boys to enjoy her charms. If their lovers could not afford to keep them in Mayfair, they occupied plain little London brick houses at Somers Town in the neighbourhood of Primrose Hill, and there was nothing shamefaced about them. They dressed well, kept their figures and their gaiety as long as they could and gave the idle gentlemen of the Regency all they asked for. They knew their place in an exclusive society where leisure, pleasure and privilege flourished as never before, and though some of them, like Harriette's youngest sister, Sophia, married into the peerage, they seldom overstepped the boundaries of the *demi-monde* to which they belonged.

They were not, of course, received at Almack's, the Assembly Rooms in King Street, St James's presided over by a cabal of ladies, whose morals were often no better than those of the *demi-reps*, but whose birth placed them in a leading position as the dictators of polite society. Grantley Berkeley described them as 'a feminine oligarchy less in number but equal in power to the Venetian Council of Ten', since they alone commanded the privilege of granting vouchers of admission to the subscription balls on Wednesday evenings; and Captain Gronow, writing fifty years later, declared: 'At the present time one can hardly conceive the importance which was attached to getting admission to Almack's, the seventh heaven of the fashionable world. Of the three hundred officers of the Foot-Guards, not more than half a dozen [of which he was one] were honoured by vouchers of admission to this exclusive temple of the *beau monde*; the gates of which were guarded by lady patronesses, whose smiles or frowns consigned men and women to happiness or despair.'

Of the seven ladies in authority, the young and beautiful sister of the future Lord Melbourne, Lady Cowper, was undoubtedly the most popular and Lady Jersey the most hated: 'her bearing was that of a theatrical tragedy queen, and whilst attempting the sublime, she frequently made herself simply ridiculous, being inconceivably rude and in her manner often ill-bred.' Lady Sefton was kind and amiable; Lady Castlereagh and Mrs Drummond-Burrell were *très grandes dames*; Princess Esterhazy a *bon enfant* and Countess Lieven haughty and exclusive.

As much intrigue went on to gain admission to this

high temple of the *ton* as was practised in the government
of the nation, and it was a hothouse of scandal and gossip,
besides being the most exigent marriage market in the
world. The balls were unexciting and the refreshments
composed of lemonade and tea, bread and butter and stale
cake, exceedingly dull. What pleasure there was consisted
wholly in the fact of being seen at Almack's in the best
and the only society that mattered or in being able to
refer casually the next morning to having spent the
evening there. Dancing was merely an alternative to
standing about and quizzing or dissecting the company
present, while attempting to shine among them; though
when Madame de Lieven and Lord Palmerston first
introduced the waltz, it caused a sensation. Some people
considered it more graceful than the country dances that
figured on the programme; others saw it as an excuse
for 'squeezing and hugging' and believed the more
sensitive ladies would faint away in horror. Byron wrote
of 'the seductive waltz . . . the voluptuous waltz',
alternately shocked and excited; and then it became a
mania. Ladies and gentlemen practised at home in the
mornings 'with unparalleled assiduity', for not to be able
to waltz after the Tsar of Russia on his visit to London
had whirled Madame de Lieven round the floor in style,
was to risk the appalling degradation of dropping out of
fashion. Even Lady Jersey danced it, not to be outdone
by the Russian Countess, with whom she kept up an
appearance of friendship although they disliked each
other 'most cordially'.

Madame de Lieven was young when she first came to
England as the wife of the Russian Ambassador. According to Charles Greville, 'she had so fine an air and
manner, and a countenance rather pretty and so full of
intelligence, as to be on the whole a very striking and
attractive person, quite enough so to have lovers, several
of whom she engaged in succession without seriously

attaching herself to any.' She almost immediately took
her place 'in the cream of the cream of English society', it
being her duty as well as her pleasure to charm the
Regent and to cultivate intimate relations with the great
political figures of her time. Thus she became the friend
of Castlereagh, Canning and the Duke of Wellington,
Lord Grey, Lord Palmerston and Lord John Russell,
winding them round her little finger with the finesse of
an accomplished foreigner, though their wives and
women friends naturally took quite a different view of
her attractions. The Duke of Wellington's intimate
friend, Mrs Arbuthnot, saw her as a devilish mistress of
intrigue, which she undoubtedly was; for waltzing at
Almack's with the distinguished men of her acquaintance
was not enough for Madame de Lieven—she wanted
power, and she got it. One great man after another
treated her as his *confidante* without apparently realizing
that to suit her own purpose or when she was bored, she
had no compunction in betraying his secrets behind his
back and that she studied to please only for what she
could gain.

No one knew better than the Countess how to titillate
the jaded appetite of the *élite*, for whom every night of the
London season was packed with fêtes and soirées, each
more modishly boring than the last. When she gave a
ball in the garden of the Russian Embassy, she displayed
the utmost ingenuity. Prince Pückler-Muskau, a visitor
from Germany, was obliged to alight 'at least a thousand
steps' from the house, as it was utterly impossible to get
through the crowd of carriages, and 'several equipages
that had tried to force their way were fast locked together,
the coachmen swearing terrible oaths at each other' in the
confusion. 'At this ball', the Prince continued, 'the hot-
houses were tapestried with moss of various hues, and
the ground thickly strewed with new-mown grass, out of
which flowers seemed to grow . . . the stalks illuminated,

which doubled the splendour of their colours. The walks were marked by coloured lamps, glittering like jewels in the grass. Gay arabesques were described among the moss on the walls . . . and in the background was a beautiful transparent landscape with moonlight and water.'

In this pleasant Arcadian setting, few could hope to resist the blandishments of the Countess. The English were really no match for her scheming subtlety. She thought they were stupid and said so; though she once admitted in a letter to her brother Count Benckendorff when he was unable to join her at Brighton, that she took pleasure in observing their way of life. 'I had fixed up in my mind', she wrote, 'that we should have travelled about together, admired together this beautiful country and these splendid country seats; and we should have laughed together at the gaucherie of their owners, but we should have agreed, as in truth I have found out, that one might gladly consent to be gauche at the price of happiness which these people enjoy and spread around them. Moreover, one finds beneath these forbidding exteriors so great a fund of good nature, cordiality, good sense, that one must sometimes shift the compliment and acknowledge oneself very gauche for having passed judgement on them.'

No doubt being fêted at Chatsworth by the Duke of Devonshire, whose establishment she found 'worthy of an Emperor', had for the moment sweetened the asperities of the Russian Ambassador's lady; it was not often that she showed much generosity of feeling towards the country that had welcomed her so warmly.

3
LIFE
in
LONDON

WHILE THE *ELITE* danced at Almack's and the dandies paraded in St James's Street, the not so exalted Londoners and visitors from the provinces found entertainment in the less fashionable quarters of the town. Vauxhall Gardens, though no longer a resort of the rich and the elegant, still attracted a vast number of pleasure seekers to its bosky and brilliantly illuminated grounds, where thousands of little coloured lamps decorated the trees and the triumphal arches, and the flimsy pavilions glittered in the evening air above cascades of water and romantic, sylvan grottoes. 'Much squealing and squalling' was heard from the girls who ventured into the notorious Dark Walk in the hope of being ambushed by the impudent young men standing about, and there were fireworks, tumblers, rope-dancers, singers, Indian jugglers and sword-swallowers to entertain, besides refreshments to be had and gewgaws to be bought at rackety prices; and at ten o'clock a grand representation of the Battle of Waterloo was staged with a thousand men and two hundred horses in action, no lack of gunpowder and shot and a scenic display which finally sent the French up in smoke and flames, much to the joy of the English spectators.

A similar show was put on at Astley's Royal Amphitheatre in Lambeth, where the spectators sat under cover and the village of Quatre Bras was shown 'partly by moonlight and partly by torch-light and fire-light'. Comic relief was introduced in the shape of performing monkeys, trick-riding, songs and pantomime; and with or without the crowning glory of Waterloo, there was always the sumptuous display of equestrian showmanship for which Astley's Royal Circus was famous. People flocked to see the lovely, bespangled Mrs Wybrow, celebrated in the arena for 'cutting and slashing with the broadsword' and out of it for her successful pursuit of no less than four husbands and quite a few lovers in between; or they drew their breath in fearful ecstasy while the enchanting young Louisa Woolford, 'a gauzy and roseate dream', danced like a second Taglioni on the back of a white circus horse. They laughed uproariously at the clownish antics of John Ducrow when he drank the contents of a bottle of wine after throwing a somersault because he had been told 'to pour it into a tumbler'; and they were thrilled by the staggering spectacle of *Mazeppa; or the Wild Horse of Tartary*, an equestrian drama devised from Byron's poem, which began in a tremendous tornado of thunder, lightning, rain and hail and went on through 'all the horrors of battle, carnage and confusion' towards a peaceful, happy ending.

Grand, spectacular effects were indeed so popular with the public at this time that the royal patent theatres of Covent Garden and Drury Lane which still enjoyed a monopoly in the legitimate drama, had to adopt them to compete with Astley's and the unlicensed theatres in the suburbs. A Shakespearian tragedy was not enough without a farce on top of it and sometimes a harlequinade, a *burletta* or a ballet in between; and at Christmas time, the pantomime at Drury Lane displayed one lavish transformation scene after another. Hazlitt, whose lifelong passion for the theatre had begun at the age of sixteen, never missed the pantomime and could never resist the playbills with 'their flaunting contents'. The length of the entertainment offered never seemed to worry him at all, neither did the extraordinary indigestibility of the programme. He loved the whole atmosphere of 'the mimic world' and saw it as a bold reflection of 'the struggle of Life and Death, the momentary pause between the cradle and the grave.'

Mrs Siddons in the days of her glory had fired his youthful imagination, stirring him to a pitch of emotional excitement that gave an extra dimension to his soul and 'filled his cup of pleasure to the full'. Looking back after her last appearance at Covent Garden, he wrote: 'She raised tragedy to the skies, or brought it down from thence. It was something above nature. . . . She was not less than a goddess or a prophetess inspired by the gods. Power was seated on her brow, passion emanated from her breast like a shrine. She was tragedy personified. . . . She was not only the idol of the people, she not only hushed the tumultuous shouts of the pit in breathless expectation, and quenched the blaze of surrounding beauty in silent tears, but to the retired and lonely student, through long years of solitude, her face has shone as if an eye had appeared from heaven, her name has been as if a voice had opened the chambers of the human heart, or as if a trumpet had awakened the sleeping and the dead.'

Mrs Siddons still had power in her voice and grandeur in her gestures, but Hazlitt regretted her appearance on this occasion when she was past her prime, and Benjamin Robert Haydon, the painter, left a somewhat more irreverent account of one of her at-homes in Baker Street where she was in the habit of giving readings from Shakespeare. 'It is extraordinary the awe this wonderful woman inspires,' he wrote. 'After her first reading the men sallied into a room to get tea. While we were all eating toast and tingling [*sic*] cups and saucers, she began again. Immediately like the effect of a Mass bell at Madrid, all noise ceased, and we slunk away to our seats like boys, two or three of the most distinguished men of the day with great bits of toast sticking out their cheeks, afraid to bite. It was curious to see Lawrence . . . his cheek swelled from his mouth being full . . . to hear him bite by degrees, and then stop for fear of making too much crackle, while his eyes full of water told the torture he was in; at the same moment you heard Mrs S say 'Eye of newt, toe of frog', then Lawrence gave a sly bite and pretended to be awed and listening. It was exquisite!'

Haydon's glee at the discomfiture of Lawrence was undoubtedly stimulated by jealousy of his fellow artist's success as a portrait painter and perhaps enlivened by the knowledge that Lawrence had already caused Mrs Siddons great anguish by transferring his affections from one of her daughters to the other, thereby destroying everyone's peace of mind and distressing the whole family. That a very unpleasant public scandal had been avoided was due entirely to the great tragedienne's immense prestige as a woman and to the respect that she and her brother, John Philip Kemble, commanded as the undisputed masters of the English stage. But time was against her and her creative spirit exhausted; and Kemble, a classical actor with a fine presence and a sonorous speaking voice, was soon to be challenged by a formidable rival.

Edmund Kean was the exact opposite of Kemble in every way. He was a little man, morose and ugly, nursing a grievance against society for the cruel years he had spent as a strolling player fighting against poverty and lack of recognition; but when at last he made his debut at Drury Lane in 1814, he took London by storm. Hazlitt, then the dramatic critic of the *Morning Chronicle*, was one of the first to respond to his genius and to assert that 'no actor had come out for many years at all to equal him'. His quick, passionate energy had not been seen since the days of Garrick; his voice, though it was harsh 'as a Hackney coachman's at one in the morning', could thunder like a god or throw away a line with devastating sweetness. His mean stature was transformed by word and gesture, and his eyes—those black eyes, 'so fierce and frightful, so tragic and so melting in their expression', had the power to mesmerize an audience. Each familiar character he portrayed, whether Shylock, Richard III or Iago, became a sudden, startling revelation of the pity and the terror of the human heart; for Kean was modern and original, and in his scornful disregard of theatrical convention, the creator of a new style. Keats declared that one of his ambitions was to make as great a revolution in modern writing as Kean had done in acting. Coleridge said: 'To see him act is like reading Shakespeare by flashes of lightning!'—and their pleasure was shared by the hundreds of playgoers who fought to get into Drury Lane.

In the theatre his magnetism never failed; he could subdue a restless audience with a glance or a gesture. Off the stage, though at last he was rich in money and courted by society, his own angry nature, scarred by the humiliations he had suffered, made him appear moody, arrogant and awkward. Invited to dine at Holland House, he was quite unable to shine among the distinguished men Lady Holland had gathered to meet him; they found him dull, ill-tempered and gauche, and his failure to impress them rankled, so that in revenge he turned to look for amusement elsewhere. Not in his home, with a wife incapable of understanding him, though determined to exploit his new prosperity in her own pretentious way, but in the taverns around Drury Lane, where he could drink and forget and behave as badly as he chose among the broken-down actors, prostitutes and perverts of the underworld who were his boozing companions. Well-meaning friends like Dr Drury, Samuel Whitbread and Douglas Kinnaird tried to save him from himself with good advice; but his personal tragedy was quite beyond their comprehension, his megalomania and his pride beyond their understanding, and the relaxation he sought in low company gradually dissipated his health and strength and finally his superb qualities as an actor.

Kean had not far to go in search of dissipation. Fashion had long ago moved away from the Covent Garden area, leaving the great houses round the Piazza to rot away or to become the haunt of every conceivable vice that went by the name of pleasure. Pierce Egan, following the fortunes of Corinthian Tom and Jerry Hawthorne among the 'Lady Birds and Debauchees' in his *Life in London*, described the scene in the saloon at Covent Garden Theatre: 'Brilliant Fanny decked out with an elegant muff and dashing plume of feathers, is skipping along to take a jelly with her old Gallant. The young *Sprig of Nobility* in black, is surveying the Brilliant as she passes him. Near to FANNY is a gay young fellow, fashionably dressed in blue, arm in arm with an antique *remnant* of fashion, one of the *Lord Ogleby* tribe, and who has been repeatedly quizzed by the Brilliant as being neither ORNAMENTAL or *useful*. But the Antique asserts, if he stays at home a single night, he is devoured with *ennui*, and that by way of apology for his appearance in the SALOON, he *merely* looks in to see an old acquaintance or if

Astley's Royal Amphitheatre
by Pugin and Rowlandson, 1808

Cremorne Pleasure Gardens in the Sixties: 'The Chinese Platform'

Ramsgate Sands
by W. P. Frith, RA, 1854

Almack's, the Temple of Exclusiveness, 1821
by I. R. and G. Cruikshank

Count D'Orsay gambling at Crockford's, 1843

anything new appears among the stock of *Frailties*. The Fair MARIA, dressed in a blue riding habit, seated on a chair in a corner near the recess and the pretty ELLEN standing behind her, are throwing out *lures* in order to attract the attention of the CORINTHIAN and JERRY. The Old Guy on the top of the stairs, with his spectacles on, fast sinking into "the lean and slippered pantaloon", is gently tapping in an amorous way, the white soft arm of lusty *black-eyed* JANE and inviting her to take a glass of wine, to which she consents in the most *business-like* manner. . . . '

And all this was in the higher strata of night life as it was lived in Covent Garden. In the stinking alleys and narrow streets round about were the sluiceries or gin-shops, a legacy from the days of Hogarth, where the mollishers 'sluiced' their throats with blue ruin or drops of jackey and the rash young bloods of the town in search of pleasure woke up to find their pockets picked or their breeches stolen and had to fight their way out of the sordid, drunken mess they had got themselves into. Not far from the old Hummums Hotel, which started as a bagnio, was the Queen's Head Tavern, where Mother Butler kept a brothel known as 'The Finish'. It remained open all through the night so that 'if shut out of your lodging', wrote Bernard Blackmantle, 'you might take shelter till morning in the *very best* of company', though Mother Butler herself was apparently a very extra-ordinary character. She was said to be witty and good-natured and to have ended her mis-spent life in respec-table retirement, unlike the hideous old Jew-women in their 'long duffle cloaks, rusty black bonnets and coloured handkerchiefs' who distressed Hazlitt so much when he saw them lurking in the lobby at Drury Lane with a crowd of young girls in their clutches, to whom they had hired out for the evening 'the trumpery clothes, curls and bracelets' of their trade.

Hazlitt's compassion for these unfortunate girls was unusual. Nearly everyone took the horrors of Covent Garden for granted and its notorious dens of iniquity did not prevent respectable people from living in the neighbourhood. Jane Austen's brother, Henry, lived above the offices of his banking house in Henrietta Street after his first wife's death and Jane often came there to stay with him. 'The house looks very nice,' she wrote to her sister Cassandra when she arrived with her favourite niece, Fanny, in September 1813, having come by coach from Chawton. 'Mde Bigeon [Henry's cook] was below dressing us a most comfortable dinner of soup, fish, bouillée, partridges and apple pie, which we sat down to soon after five, after cleaning and dressing ourselves and feeling that we were most commodiously disposed of.' They went to the theatre that evening for a performance of *Don Juan* and out the next morning before breakfast to Layton & Shear's, the fashionable mercers in Henrietta Street, where Jane saw some 'very pretty English poplins at 4s 3d and some Irish ditto at 6s, more pretty, certainly'—and very tempting.

To any woman up from the country the smart shops in London were a tremendous attraction. They offered a variety of exciting things: silk stockings, French gloves, satins and brocades, Indian muslins, tippets of fur and feather, plumes of all kinds, ribbons and lace and fancy trimmings in the latest mode. Jane was glad to learn from her dressmaker, Mrs Tickars, that 'the stays now are not made to force the bosom up at all—a very unbecoming, unnatural fashion', and that gowns were not worn 'so much off the shoulder as they were'; and Miss Hare, the milliner, had some 'pretty caps', which she agreed to copy in white satin and lace with 'a little white flower perking out of the left ear.' Jane cautiously allowed the milliner 'to go as far as 36s' for the cap with the white flower, but became much more extravagant when her other brother,

Edward, gave her five pounds to spend, hurrying back
to Layton & Shear's, where she treated herself to twenty
yards of striped poplin. Later she spoke of seeing 'a
great many pretty caps in the windows of Cranbourn
Alley' and of ruining herself 'in sattin ribbon with a
proper perl edge'. The shops, in fact, were the highlight
of her visits to London, and when Henry took her to
Drury Lane a year later to see Kean as Shylock, like
everyone else she was so carried away, she thought there
was 'no fault in him anywhere'.

Henry Austen was a regular theatre-goer, and he was
not the only man of good character to live within walking
distance of Drury Lane. Charles Lamb and his sister Mary
moved to Russell Street from the Inner Temple in 1817,
and in a joint letter to Dorothy Wordsworth expressed
their pleasure in being there. 'We are in the individual
spot I like best in all this great city,' Charles wrote. 'The
theatres with all their noises. Covent Garden, dearer to
me than any Garden of Alcinous, where we are morally
sure of the earliest peas and 'sparagus. Bow Street where
the thieves are examined within a few yards of us. Mary
had not been here four and twenty hours before she saw a
Thief. She sits at the window working, and casually
throwing out her eyes, she sees a concourse of people
coming this way, with a constable to conduct the solem-
nity. These little incidents agreeably diversify a female
life.' And Mary in the same letter declared that the noise
of the carriages returning from the play did not annoy
her in the least. 'I quite enjoy looking out of the window
and listening to the calling up of the carriages and the
squabbles of the coachmen and link-boys,' she added. 'It
is the oddest scene to look down upon.'

Tied by his work as a clerk at East India House and by
his ever watchful care of his dear sister, Lamb had very
little leisure to pursue his favourite interests and once
complained of not being able 'to keep a holyday now

once in ten times, where I used to keep all red-letter days
and some days besides.' Yet it was here, in Russell
Street, that he began to write the *Essays of Elia*, and here
that he entertained his friends at his Wednesday evening
parties. No pleasure in life was so sweet to him as friendship, and with his gentle, affectionate nature and his
extraordinary understanding of his fellow men, he had a
genius for it. Coleridge, Wordsworth, Southey, Godwin,
Leigh Hunt and Hazlitt might quarrel among themselves
—they often did; but they never quarrelled with Lamb,
or not for long. His detachment from the political con-
troversies of the day often made him the peace-maker
among them, for with a warmth of feeling that endeared
him to everyone, he never failed to find the right word
or to draw his friends together. At his 'Wednesdays', the
cards for cribbage or whist were laid out on the mahogany
table with a snuff-box for communal use in one corner
and a cold supper ready on the side-board. Punch or
brandy and water helped to loosen the tongue, and as the
night went on into the small hours of the morning there
was often 'a flight of high and earnest talk that took one
half-way to the stars'.

A very little alcohol went to Lamb's head and stimulated his sense of fun. At the 'Immortal Dinner' Haydon
gave at his studio when he was painting his vast canvas of
Christ's Entry into Jerusalem, he got 'excessively merry
and exquisitely witty, and his fun,' according to Haydon,
'in the midst of Wordsworth's solemn intonations of
oratory was like the sarcasm and wit of the fool in the
intervals of Lear's passion.' The other guests—Keats and
Thomas Monkhouse, a kinsman of Wordsworth's—
egged him on, and 'it was delightful,' Haydon continued,
'to see the good-humour of Wordsworth in giving in to
all our frolics without affectation and laughing as
heartily as the rest of us.'

Another guest, by the name of Kingston, who came in

late, was less appreciative of the high jinks going on. Being sober, he addressed himself chiefly to Wordsworth in a stiff, uncompromising manner, which encouraged Lamb to make such glorious fun of him that Keats and Haydon had to bundle their irresponsible companion into another room, where they all three gave way to 'inextinguishable laughter'. But Wordsworth's fine intonation as he quoted Milton and Virgil, 'like the funeral bell of St Paul's and the music of Handel mingled', Lamb's sparkling wit and Keats's 'rich fancy of Satyrs and Fauns and doves and white clouds' so speeded the stream of conversation that Haydon declared he had never in all his life passed such a delightful time. 'With my Picture of Christ's Entry towering up behind them and occasionally brightened by the gleam of flame that sparkled from the fire,' he concluded, 'it was a night worthy of the Elizabethan age and will long flash upon "that inward eye which is the bliss of solitude".'

Haydon planned to put portraits of all his friends into his great picture in the style of the High Renaissance which he admired so much, but like so many of his ambitious projects, the picture hung fire, and he was apt to quarrel with anyone who dared to question his grandiose ideas. Nevertheless he had an enormous zest for life and a great capacity for enjoying it, and the encouragement he gave to Keats at this time was vital to the twenty-one-year-old poet. It was Haydon who first took Keats to see the Parthenon sculptures brought over to England by Lord Elgin, an experience that moved the poet to ecstasy; and it was with Haydon that Keats stayed up late into the night 'spouting Shakespeare' until he was intoxicated. Haydon shared his enthusiasms, stimulated his idealism and gave him confidence in himself when he was most in need of it; and it was not the fault of Keats that he was unable to come to the assistance of his friend with a loan some two years later: it was simply that he had no money of his own and could not raise another penny from any of his friends.

Keats lodged in Hampstead, then a village on the unspoilt rural fringe of London: at first in Well Walk with his two brothers Tom and George, and after Tom's death, with his friend Charles Armitage Brown at Wentworth Place, next door to Mrs Brawne and her daughter Fanny. In Well Walk before Tom's illness cast a shadow over their gaiety, the three brothers made their own amusements, giving hilarious 'concerts' in which each took the part of a different instrument, Keats imitating the bassoon and Haydon the organ; and although the air of Hampstead failed to strengthen poor Tom, the lyrical beauty of its landscape was a constant joy to his brother. He took long walks over the Heath to Lord Mansfield's park at Caen Wood, or went down the hill to the Vale of Health to visit Leigh Hunt in his cottage there. 'I found the young poet's heart as warm as his imagination,' Hunt wrote. 'We read and walked together, and used to write verses of an evening on a given subject. No imaginative pleasure was left unnoticed by us, or unenjoyed; from the recollections of the bards and patriots of old, to the luxury of a summer rain on our window, or the clicking of the coal in wintertime.' And Keats himself, although his youthful hero-worship of Hunt diminished as he grew older, never forgot those blissful evenings, when Hunt's 'matchless conversation' filled him with excitement and hope for the future.

At Wentworth Place, restless and ill, he watched his hope gradually receding. Yet there was pleasure here, too, in the spring of 1819, when a nightingale built her nest in the garden. 'Keats felt a tranquil and continual joy in her song,' Brown wrote, 'and one morning he took his chair from the breakfast table to the grass-plot under the plum-tree, where he sat for two or three hours. When he came into the house I perceived he had some scraps of paper in his hands and these he was quietly thrusting behind some books.' Thus the radiant *Ode to a Nightingale* was written and all the sweetness and the bitterness of life resolved in the poet's cathartic longing for repose:

> Now more than ever seems it rich to die,
>   To cease upon the midnight with no pain,
>   While thou art pouring forth thy soul abroad
>   In such an ecstasy!

Brown had a great affection for Keats and had been a gay companion on the walking tour they took together in the Lake District. Kind and good-natured, though somewhat lacking in imagination, he did his best to look after the poet when he became too ill to go out of the house and when his only remaining pleasure was to watch for Fanny Brawne as she passed his window. 'I think you had better not make any long stay with me when Mr Brown is at home,' he wrote in one of his notes to her. 'Whenever he goes out you may bring you work. You will have a pleasant walk today. I shall see you pass. . . . ' Then he begged her: 'Come round to my window when you have read this'—a request which Fanny could not refuse. Not yet twenty, with a fondness for pretty clothes and gay parties, poor Fanny tried to please him and to comfort him. She came and sat with him when Brown was out and put on warm clothes when he told her to, and perhaps she tried to make him believe there was still some future for them; but Keats knew when he left Hampstead in the autumn of 1820 for his journey to Italy that he would never see her or Wentworth Place again.

Hampstead had once been a fashionable pleasure haunt and its chalybeate springs famous for their healing qualities, but the Assembly Rooms in Well Walk, built in the time of Queen Anne, were now derelict and forsaken. Its good air, however, and its wonderful situation on the hills overlooking the whole panorama of London, still appealed to those in search of health, besides offering them all the delights of the country within a short coach ride from the city. For John Constable, who first took his wife and children there in the same year that Keats left Wentworth Place, it was ideal as a retreat in the summer from the suffocating heat of central London. In fact, he and his wife came to love Hampstead so much, they eventually settled in a comfortable little house in Well Walk. 'We are once more enjoying our own furniture and sleeping on our own beds,' he told his friend Fisher. 'My plans in search of health for my family have been ruinous; but I hope now that our movable camp no longer exists and that I am settled for life. . . . This house is indeed everything we can wish. It is my wife's heart's content . . . and our little drawing-room commands a view unequalled in Europe—from Westminster Abbey to Gravesend. The dome of St Paul's in the air realizes Michael Angelo's idea on seeing that of the Pantheon—"I will build such a thing in the sky"—and we see the woods and lofty grounds of the East Saxons to the north-east.'

Constable was far too occupied in trying to make both ends meet to have any leisure at his disposal. But still in love with his native Suffolk, the county that made him a painter, and prevented by his busy life in London from returning there very often, he found Hampstead with its wonderful views a compensation and a rich source of inspiration; and it was here that he made some of his most beautiful outdoor sketches, especially of the ever changing skies over his favourite landscape from the Upper Heath. 'We have had noble clouds and effects of light and dark and color,' he wrote in another letter to Fisher. 'Independent of my *jobs* [the commissions he undertook to make money] I have done some studies and made many skies and effects. . . . ' And there was one day in October 'so lovely that I could not paint for looking,'

he added. 'My wife was walking with me all the middle of
the day on the beautiful heath.'

Such simple pleasures gave Constable great joy. He
cared nothing for the idleness and the extravagance of the
Regency, and his painting was too far ahead of its time
to attract the kind of patronage which would have given
him freedom from his perpetual financial anxiety, while
his fellow artists, jealous of their own advancement,
failed to appreciate his extraordinary gifts. His election
to the Royal Academy came late and did little to com-
pensate him for the neglect he had suffered; nevertheless
he could still declare: 'I have a kingdom both fertile and
populous—my landscape and my children. I am envied
by many and much richer people'—and it was a kingdom
he loved dearly. When he was separated from his wife,
even while staying with his good friend Fisher at Salisbury, he wrote: 'I hope nothing will prevent me from
seeing you on Sunday . . . I am quite home sick (perhaps
love-sick) and for my darling babies. I am uncomfortable
away so long.'

Not a day passed that he did not think of Maria with
affection or strive to increase her happiness, and when
her illness and death in 1828 overwhelmed him with
grief, it was to his seven young children that he turned
for comfort. Henceforth their wellbeing was his first
consideration and he never allowed anything to stand
between him and his enjoyment of their growing companionship. He took the boys to Suffolk where they
'ranged the woods and fields and searched the crag-pits
for shells', and he was proud of his pretty little girls with
their gay young faces and their accomplishments. Young
and excitable, they were equally devoted to him; and
when he took them about with him on his journeys by
coach, riding outside with the sky above them and the
wind in their faces, they shared his delight in the beauty
of the lush green fields and the water meadows, the

opulent corn and the tall trees that he was forever observing with the sharp eye of an artist and the simple heart of an Englishman born and bred in the country.

4

RURAL
PLEASURES

VISITORS TO ENGLAND at this time, even if they lacked
the vision of her greatest landscape painter, were all
tremendously impressed by the beauty of the country.
For the first time in history, travelling for pleasure had
been made easy by the fast mail and stage coaches running
at speed on the smooth roads of Telford and Macadam.
Passengers riding outside, if they did not mind the
vagaries of the weather, had a wonderful view of the
countryside, and never before had they seen such superb
houses or so many of them set in the ravishing green of
their surrounding parks, where the deer browsed in the
shade of the tall trees, peacocks strutted about the lawns,
and the dogs and the horses had as many servants to look
after them as their owners could command indoors. The
great architects and landscape gardeners of the eighteenth
century had immeasurably improved the whole aspect of
the country, and the taste and judgement of their noble
patrons had never before reached such a high aesthetic
standard. In garden design no nation in the world could
equal the achievements of the English; and within their

houses, elegance and beauty were combined with comfort for a whole generation, to whom encouragement of the arts and literature, gambling, politics, a zeal for outdoor sports and an absorbing interest in new agricultural methods were concomitant with life lived on the most extravagant scale. Leisure and pleasure were united in an infinite variety of ways and were a distinctive part of the wealthy landowners' inheritance.

Richard Rush, the American Ambassador to Britain in 1819, observed that 'the permanent interests and affections of the most opulent classes centre almost universally in the country. They have *houses* in London, in which they stay while Parliament sits and occasionally visit at other seasons; but their *homes* are in the country . . . where they flourish in pomp and joy.' Hence the complete desertion of the West End when Parliament rose and everyone of importance returned home as quickly as possible. Not that the cessation of parliamentary business at Westminster meant the end of political jobbery; for the policies and the appointments of the two great opposing parties continued to be discussed and decided over the port and the brandy in the vast, ornate dining-rooms of the great country mansions, where the Whig and Tory lords lived *en prince* and entertained a perpetual stream of visitors.

Some of the guests enjoyed themselves—others did not; it depended on who was there. When Charles Greville visited Belvoir Castle on the Duke of Rutland's birthday, the party was 'very large and sufficiently dull'. Apart from the Duke of Wellington and one or two others, they were 'a rabble of fine people, without beauty or wit among them'; and the splendour of the establishment, where a different display of plate appeared on the table every evening for dinner and the guests were roused in the morning by martial music played by the band of the Duke's own regiment on the terrace outside their windows, was no compensation for the dullness of the company.

More fun was evidently to be had below stairs in this lordly castle, for the Duke's birthday was a very merry occasion in the servants' hall. One hundred and forty-five servants sat down to dinner and were not only drinking the Duke's health when Greville looked in on them, but 'singing and speechifying with vociferous applause, shouting and clapping of hands . . . the palm of eloquence being universally conceded to Mr Tapps, the head coachman, a man of great abdominal dignity, whose Ciceronian brows were adorned with an ample flaxen wig.' Greville thought it would be a good idea if some of the surly Radicals who snarled at the selfish aristocracy for having no sympathies with the poor, were to witness this scene of rejoicing and the way it was continued in the villages round about with beef and ale at the Duke's expense, music and dancing and the ringing of the church bells throughout the Vale of Belvoir. 'The Duke,' he concluded, 'is as selfish a man as any of his class—that is, he never does what he does not like and spends his whole life in a round of such pleasures as suit his taste, but he is neither a foolish nor a bad man, and partly from a sense of duty, partly from inclination, he devotes time and labour to the interest and the welfare of the people who live and labour on his estate.'

And it was the same at Chatsworth, where the young Duke of Devonshire had not long succeeded to his rich inheritance. Here Greville enjoyed himself and was much happier. 'The party was immense,' he wrote. 'Forty people sat down to dinner every day, and about 150 servants in the steward's room and servants' hall. Nothing could be more agreeable from the gaiety of numbers and the entire liberty that prevails; all the resources of the house—horses, carriages, keepers etc—are placed at the disposal of the guests, and everyone does

what they like best. In the evening they acted charades
or danced, and there was plenty of whist and *écarté* high
and low.' But Greville's good opinion of the Duke's
hospitality was not shared by another of the visitors to
Chatsworth, the gay and attractive sister of Lord Auck-
land, Emily Eden, who went there in 1825. 'You are
probably right in thinking the Duke takes pleasure in
making people do what they don't like,' she wrote to
her friend Miss Villiers, 'and that accounts for his asking
me so often. We have now made a rule to accept one
invitation out of two. We go there with the best disposi-
tions, wishing to be amused, liking the people we meet
there . . . supported by the knowledge that in the eyes of
the neighbourhood we are covering ourselves with glory
by frequenting the *great house*; but with all these helps
we have never been able to stay above two days there
without finding change of air absolutely necessary—
never could turn the corner of the third day—at the end
of the second the great depths of *bore* were broken up
and carried all before them: we were obliged to pretend
that some christening, or a grand funeral, or some
pressing case of wedding required our immediate return
home, and so we departed yawning.'

Emily, no doubt, found Chatsworth a strain because
the Duke was a bachelor. She was so devoted to her
brother, she resisted all the attempts of her match-making
friends to marry her off, asserting some years later when
she was thirty-five, that she was then too old for Lord
Melbourne, who had just lost his troublesome wife
Caroline and was paying her a great deal of attention.
'Though I am sure it is very kind of my friends to wish
me married,' she wrote, 'and particularly kind that anybody should wish to marry me, yet I think now they may
give it up, and give me credit for knowing my own
happiness. . . . If I were younger or less spoiled than I
have been at home, I daresay I could put up with the

difficulties of a new place; but not now. I cannot be blind
to the faults of the few men I know well, and though I
know many more faults in myself, yet I am used to those,
you know, and George is used to them and it does
beautifully.' In this, as in everything else, though it was
for her time a very unorthodox point of view, Emily had
the satisfaction of knowing her own mind. When she was
twenty-one, she judged one of her admirers by his
trousers. 'As for your friend Mr Graham,' she wrote to
her brother, 'though I do not wish to be severe, yet I
cannot think a man who wears a light sort of mulberry-
coloured "don't mentions", from a wish to look *waspish*,
can be any great shakes.'

Boring company, in whatever coloured trousers, was
utterly intolerable to Emily, but she enjoyed the intellectual amusements in some of the country houses she
visited. The amateur theatricals at Hatfield were fun—she
had never laughed 'more heartily' at any play so well
acted; and she found Panshanger, the castellated Gothic
mansion of Lord and Lady Cowper, 'full to the brim of
vice and agreeableness, foreigners and roués', including
Lord Alvanley, who was more amusing than ever. All the
guests here knew each other very well, and it was the
same at Lord Grantham's house, Newby Hall, which was
'excessively comfortable, with a stove in every passage,
and a fire in every room . . . an excellent library, and a very
pretty statue gallery, heaps of amusing books, and an
armchair for every limb.' Lord Grantham amused himself with his own private puppet theatre, everyone
helping him to make the dolls and dress them, and he
liked listening to Emily playing the piano for hours
together. Lady Grantham was an enthusiastic gardener and had a taste for informality, which Emily
shared, so that when most of the guests had gone,
she found it 'uncommonly pleasant, after so much
company, to be able to go about the house with

EASTON PUBLIC LIBRARY
EASTON PA

rough hair, or a *tumbled* frill and in an old black gown.'

Bowood in Wiltshire, the home of Lord Lansdowne and his beautiful wife, was another house Emily liked visiting. After a fortnight there, she wrote: 'The house was full of people and we enjoyed ourselves amazingly. It is always rather surprising society in point of talk; there is less said about people, and more about books than in most country houses'; and she was fascinated by Lady Lansdowne's experiments with 'some receipts for dyeing muslins, sattins and silks any colours', observing that 'she has been all the morning up to the elbows in soap-suds, starch and blue, and then on her knees for an hour ironing on the floor'—a most unusual kind of amusement for the lady of the house, and a marchioness at that.

Yet it was, perhaps, not very easy for the ladies to find their own amusements when their menfolk went off hunting and shooting all day long. With an army of servants to wait on them, a steward, a chef and a house-keeper, they were practically free of all domestic responsibility and their leisure was interminable. No wonder they gobbled up the romantic novels of Sir Walter Scott and thrilled to the poetry of Byron, while they nibbled com-fits and sat for hours at their morning toilet. They toyed a little with their children and their dogs, and sometimes, for want of excitement, fell in love with their boys' tutor or someone else's husband. Some of them wrote poetry and took music or dancing lessons from visiting Italian music masters with tiny waists and black curly hair, or they studied Greek and Latin as an excuse to flirt with their lord's librarian. They took endless pleasure in gossip and in damaging each other's reputation; and they went out, of course, riding and driving to take the air and visit their neighbours; but sport was largely the prerogative of the male and with most men an obsession. Shooting was the exclusive privilege of the rich land-

owners and their invited guests, a fact which, combined
with the antiquated game laws of the land, caused great
bitterness in the country and led to the terrible poaching
war of the 1820s. The individual sportsman out with his
gun and his dog for a day's pleasure in the fields had
fallen a victim to the eighteenth-century enclosure of
the countryside and, with the development of the *battue*
or system of beaters driving the birds towards the guns,
large shooting parties had now come into fashion as a
major form of entertainment for the gentry. These were
highly organized affairs under the command of the host
and his head gamekeeper with a regiment of under-
keepers and rustics from the village to act as loaders and
beaters. Some gentlemen, no doubt, were glad of the
advice given to the gamekeepers in a shooting manual
of the time, which said: 'Do not forget the sandwich case
and flask of brandy to hand to the gentlemen, when their
nerves get a little affected. Assist them in reloading,
during which time let them stand as still as possible, till
they get quite cool and collected. The trembling being
quite off, proceed very deliberately.'

Accidents did happen to mar the day's pleasure. The
Duke of Wellington at Wherstead 'peppered Lord
Granville's face with nine shot', fortunately missing his
eyes but giving him great pain, according to Lady
Cowper, who dismissed the incident as 'unlucky'.
Another time at Ashridge, when the Duke of York was
of the party, Wellington's aim was a good deal better.
His double-barrelled gun was said to have brought down
everything before it, and in three days the eight sports-
men in the party fired 1,971 shots and killed 1,088 head of
game. Such enormous bags were a status symbol among
the landowners and it became necessary for them to start
rearing pheasants on their grounds to provide enough
birds for the season's massacre. The Dukes of Richmond,
Marlborough and Bedford began the practice of buying

pheasants' eggs and employing more and more keepers to look after them, and before long the passion for shooting among the gentry spread to Scotland, Emily Eden reporting in August 1824 that her brother had gone there to 'kill the poor dumb grouse—or grice, as they ought to be in the plural'. When he almost blew his fingers off, she took it very calmly.

Hunting, in spite of its perils, was less hazardous than shooting and a sport which caused far less bad blood among the country people. For one thing it could be enjoyed by everyone, even the onlooker on foot, to whom the horses and hounds and gay-coated huntsmen on a bright winter's morning were a spectacle that gave great delight; for another, it had by now developed into the national sport of a generation whose love of horses did not stop this side of idolatry.

In the shires, huge sums of money were spent by those who hunted with the Quorn, the Pytchley, the Cottesmore and the Belvoir, and Melton Mowbray became the resort of 'persons of rank, wealth and fashion, who, during the winter months, resigned the comforts and elegancies of their family mansions for a small house, in order to enjoy six days a week in the hunting-field'. Harriette Wilson, who once followed her rich sugar baker, Mr Meyler, there, did not think anything of their sottish behaviour or of the loose women hanging about outside and tapping on the window pane in their efforts to vie with the fox for the hunting gentlemen's favours. But Melton did very well out of the gentlemen, who spent some £50,000 a year in the town and were to be seen mounted on the finest hunters in the world. Thomas Assheton-Smith, a Member of Parliament, who was also a man of science, a noted athlete and 'the straightest man across country that ever rode to hounds' was master of the Quorn from 1806 to 1817; and he was followed by an equally famous gentleman huntsman, 'Squire' Osbaldeston, whose passionate love of the chase was only matched by his capacity for riding in cross-country races and gambling heavily on them.

It was not, however, absolutely necessary to be a Croesus to enjoy fox-hunting. The invaluable Mr Tilbury of Mount Street was ready to hire out 'two good hunters with a clean obliging servant and every requisite for the horses, and pay all expenses, for 40 guineas a month, with the servant's expenses included'; and this was quite a bargain, since if either of the horses went lame, Tilbury at once replaced it and sent the damaged animal off to recuperate on his farm at Pinner. Even the extravagant C. J. Apperley, who wrote for *The Sporting Magazine* under the pseudonym of 'Nimrod' and managed to squeeze £1,500 a year out of the editor for his expenses, was mounted by Tilbury on some of his hunting tours which took him all round the country; and almost anyone who could afford to hire a horse or to saddle one of his own, from the village parson and the local farmers to the 'new men' from London and the provincial towns now making money out of trade, was able to enjoy the chase at one time or another. Mr Jorrocks, the vulgar and lovable city grocer created by Surtees, was the epitome of all the new men who took to fox-hunting, and he summed up the excitement to be derived from it when he declared: 'It's the dash of the 'ound, the feathering for the scent, the picking it out, the challenge when it's found, the rush of the pack to the cry—the werry sight of the beauteous mottled intelligent h'animals is enough to set my werry blood boiling.'

Mr Jorrocks and his kind were accepted by some of the subscription packs which came into existence at this time, though Mrs Jorrocks would not have been. Women in the hunting-field were not looked upon with any great favour until a good deal later in the century. Hounds were much faster than ever before and the new fashion for galloping at fences was considered very risky for anyone riding side-saddle, attired in the beplumed hats and voluminous riding-habits still *de rigeuer* for the ladies. The solitary exception was the Marchioness of Salisbury, who, as master of the Hatfield Hunt from 1775 until 1819 when she became so blind she had to be tied on to her horse, could out-ride and outwit any gentleman in the field. 'Women generally ride like the devil,' Surtees remarked. 'They either "go" to beat the men or they don't "go" at all', and they spoilt the pleasure of the hunting men by making them feel awkward if they went ahead and left them in the lurch—unless, of course, the women happened to be young and pretty. Then they could do as they pleased. 'Dishevelled hair, ruddy and perspiring face and muddy habit,' Surtees added, 'are more likely to be forgiven in the bloom of youth than in what ought to be the sobriety of maturer years.'

When the hunting season was over, the racing season began and the sporting gentlemen of rank and fashion moved from Melton Mowbray to Newmarket, which had been a great centre for horse-racing ever since King James I made it popular in 1605. The headquarters of the Jockey Club were there and everyone foregathered in the Coffee Room, where bets were laid on the horses and gambling at cards continued from morning till night. Sir Charles Bunbury was one of the stewards from 1768 until his death at the age of eighty-one in 1821; but his obsessive love of sport was not at all to the taste of his first wife, Lady Sarah Lennox, the lovely young daughter of the Duke of Richmond, who found country life in Suffolk intolerably dull. 'To tell you about the fair,' she wrote to a friend, 'I hate it all and am tired to death, but as I know you expect more you must have it all with the faults of my description. *In primis*, Lord Ossory is with us, and went to the Assembly; he is an agreeable man and I like him vastly . . . I danced with Lord Petre and he is a nasty toad for I long'd to spit in his face . . . The agreeable Mr Shute was so drunk last night that he swore at his partner, Mrs Harland, till she left him and took another. You need not have envied me, for my devil of a horse is as lame as a dog, and Mr B. [Bunbury had not yet succeeded to the baronetcy] has been coursing, hunting and doing every pleasant thing upon earth, and poor me sat fretting and fuming at home with Lady Rosse.'

'Poor me' did not endure her rural isolation for very long. After five years she ran away from Newmarket with Lord William Gordon, and Bunbury, who knew less of his wife's affairs than anyone else in the neighbourhood, was advised not to challenge Gordon to a duel, since he could be numbered as the tenth of Lady Sarah's lovers and Bunbury would have needed to fight all the other nine before he took on Gordon. Bunbury therefore gave up the idea and returned to his first love for consolation, being a better judge of a horse than of a spirited young lady.

His racing stables were on a relatively modest scale compared with those of the Dukes of Richmond, Bedford and Grafton, or the Earls of Jersey, Egremont and Derby; and he kept his gambling within sensible limits, though he was not as abstemious as the Duke of Portland, who never laid a bet, but from a purely disinterested love of racing, did much to improve its standards. He had a great wagon fitted up as a movable stand, from which he could watch through his telescope any part of the course while the races were going on, and as the owner of a large area of Newmarket Heath, he set to work at his own expense clearing acres of furze and scrub and laying down grass as a training ground for the horses stabled in the neighbourhood.

Prince Pückler-Muskau was astonished by the number of race horses to be seen exercising on the rising ground at Newmarket in the early morning. 'The bare, widespread heath is covered with them as with a herd of cattle,' he wrote. 'Some are walking at a foot pace, others galloping, some slower, some quicker, but none at full speed. . . . All are ridden without a saddle by little half-dressed lads, one of whom is every now and then thrown, for the amusement of the spectators.' And after this, the Prince reported: 'People breakfast and in half an hour go to the sale, which takes place almost every day in the open street, under the auspices of the far famed Mr Tattersall. They then ride or drive to the races.'

All along the course the Prince observed rows of carriages three or four deep, standing without their horses and crowded from top to bottom with spectators, while the excitement at the betting-post was something he had never witnessed anywhere before. 'In noise, uproar and clamour, the scene resembles a Jews' synagogue, with a greater display of passion. The persons of the drama are the first peers of England, livery-servants, the lowest sharpers and black-legs; in short, all who have money to bet here claim equal rights; nor is there any marked difference in their external appearance. Dukes, lords, grooms and rogues shout, scream and halloo together, and bet together . . . till suddenly the cry is heard: "The horses have started!" In a minute the crowd disperses; but the bettors soon meet again at the ropes which enclose the course. You see a multitude of telescopes, opera-glasses and eyeglasses levelled from the carriages and by the horsemen in the direction whence the jockeys are coming . . . and for a few moments a deep and anxious silence pervades the motley crowd, while a manager on horseback keeps the course clear and applies his whip without ceremony to the shoulders of any intruder. . . . Then once more arises the wildest uproar: shouts and lamentations, curses and cheers re-echo on every side, from Lords and Ladies, far and wide. "Ten to four on the Admiral! A hundred to one on Madame Vestris! Small Beer against the field!" are heard from the almost frantic bettors; and scarcely do you hear a "Done!" uttered here and there, when the noble animals are before you—past you—in the twinkling of an eye; the next moment at the goal, and luck or skill or knavery have decided the victory.'

The Prince backed a winner on his first day at New-market, gaining a considerable sum of money, which he lost the next day and more besides; but he never lost his amazement at the sporting habits of the English. To him, as the hereditary ruler of a small principality in Germany, it was inconceivable that the English aristocracy could share their pleasure in horse-racing on equal terms with the mob; and it was the same with prize-fighting, the even more popular sport of the Regency, which induced the highest and the lowest in the land to mingle together to a degree quite unknown on the Continent. The great pugilists of the day—Tom Cribb and Belcher, Savage Shelton and the terrible Randall, Ned Turner, Tom Spring, Gully and the Chicken, the Gas-man and Bill Neate—enjoyed a national prestige equal to the exploits of Wellington in the field of battle. The noble lords, who promoted the fights, were proud to be seen driving these celebrated 'bruisers' in their carriages or hob-nobbing with them before they entered the ring. Byron travelled down to Brickhill in a barouche-and-four, with Gentle-man Jackson and a party of friends, to watch the fight between Gully and the Chicken; and when Hazlitt went down to Hungerford to see the fight between Bill Neate and the Gas-man, hundreds of carriages, carts and wagons passed him on the road, all converging on the ring.

It was a fine December morning. 'The grass was wet, and the ground miry and ploughed up with multitudinous feet, except that within the ring itself, there was a spot of virgin-green closed in and unprofaned by vulgar tread, that shone with dazzling brightness in the mid-day sun.' The excitement was intense. £200,000 was at stake and some 20,000 spectators were waiting for their idols to appear. Bill Neate 'rolled along, swathed in his loose great coat, his knock knees bending under his huge bulk; and with a modest and cheerful air, threw his hat into the ring. . . . The Gas-man came forward with a conscious air of anticipated triumph, too much like the cock-of-the-walk.' Then they stripped, tossed up for the sun, shook hands and went at it. At first the Gas-man had it all his own way and 'flew at his adversary like a tiger', and Neate fell down, 'a mighty ruin'. But he recovered himself and started punishing the Gas-man hard, and sent him down while the spectators roared their approval. Blood poured down the Gas-man's face and his right eye closed 'in a dingy blackness'. But what Hazlitt and the punch-drunk rabble admired was the courage of the two combatants: to see them 'smashed to the ground, smeared with gore, stunned, senseless, the breath beaten out of their bodies; and then to see them rise up with new strength and courage, stand ready to inflict or receive mortal offence, and rush upon each other "like two clouds over the Caspian".' This was the most astonishing thing of all—'the high and heroic state of man!' When at last the Gas-man was battered beyond recovery, carrier pigeons were sent off to Mrs Neate with the news of her husband's victory.

But the colossal sums of money wagered on the prize-fights attracted all the scum of the sporting world and before long even the patronage of the swells in their white box-coats failed to keep the fighting clean. Crossing or tampering with a fight became the common practice and when the ring degenerated into a general scrimmage, the orgiastic violence of the spectators, pushing and shouting and kicking in a delirium of savage excitement, spoilt the pleasure of the more sensitive men like Hazlitt. By 1831 prize-fighting had sunk so low, it was listed by Surtees among the demoralizing pursuits such as cock-fighting and bull-baiting, which he refused to notice in his *New Sporting Magazine*, and four years later it was made illegal. The Methodist preachers of the industrial towns, who saw in the uninhibited lust for pleasure of the Regency the work of the devil, had won their first victory against the country gentry and the mob. Times were changing. The First Gentleman in Europe was dead, and his brother, King William IV, had only two more years to live.

5

QUEEN VICTORIA

and

PRINCE ALBERT

ON 20 JUNE 1837, Charles Greville, as clerk to the Privy Council, repaired to Kensington Palace to attend the first meeting of Queen Victoria with her councillors. 'There never was anything like the first impression she produced,' he wrote, 'or the chorus of praise and admiration which is raised about her manner and her behaviour. . . . Her extreme youth and inexperience, and the ignorance of the world concerning her, naturally excited intense curiosity to see how she would act on this trying occasion.' All the great officers of state were present: the

Archbishops, Lord Melbourne as Prime Minister, the Duke of Wellington, Lord Grey, Lord Brougham, Sir Robert Peel and the two surviving Royal Dukes, Cumberland and Sussex. All had tears in their eyes—not of regret for the King who was dead, but of sentimental tenderness for the blue-eyed young girl who was now their Queen.

She was plainly dressed, in deep mourning, and her conduct was beyond reproach: graceful and engaging, calm and self-possessed, with a decorum and a modesty which contrasted very strongly with the total lack of dignity shown on every possible occasion by her uncle, the late King William IV. 'Since it has pleased Providence to place me in this station,' she wrote in her diary that evening, 'I shall do my utmost to fulfil my duty towards my country; I am very young and perhaps in many, though not in all things, inexperienced, but I am sure that very few have more real good will and more real desire to do what is fit and right than I have.' And so it was to be—to the very end as it was in the beginning: except that what was fit and right in the Queen's opinion tended to harden as the years went on into an obstinate, self-willed egotism.

Now, however, she was still eighteen and had only just emerged from the domineering shadow of her mother the Duchess of Kent, to be Queen of England and her own mistress at last. She was not a beauty; her blue eyes were rather prominent, her small teeth protruded over her lower lip and her chin receded. But she had a fresh pink and white complexion and a pleasing manner, and her natural high spirits appealed to everyone. 'A more homely little being you never beheld, *when she is at her ease*, and she is evidently dying to be more so,' old Creevey declared. 'She laughs in real earnest, opening her mouth as wide as it can go, showing not very pretty gums. . . . She eats quite as heartily as she laughs, I think

I may say she gobbles. She blushes and laughs every instant in so natural a way as to disarm anybody.' She was, in fact, enjoying herself immensely in a simple, girlish way: enjoying her new importance, her popularity and her power after a not very happy and very secluded childhood constantly disturbed by her mother's quarrelsome nature. Full of vitality and quick to learn, she at last had a chance to use her abundant energy to some purpose, and far from being frightened by those bulky red leather boxes stuffed to the brim with affairs of state, she revelled in them. 'I get so many papers to sign every day, that I have a *very great* deal to do,' she wrote in her journal, adding, 'I *delight* in the work', and again, 'I receive so many communications from my Ministers, but I like it very much.'

She liked her first Prime Minister, Lord Melbourne, too. Indeed it was more than liking. In a very short time he was her 'dear Lord M.' and she adored him, which was not surprising. He was witty and wise and fascinating; old enough to be her father, young enough still to be flattered by her devotion and to take pleasure in the intimacy that quickly developed between them; sensible enough to modify his own behaviour to suit the innocence of the immature girl, who was both his royal mistress and his pupil. With his profound experience of the world, his aristocratic good looks, his knowledge of women and his charm, he knew exactly how to amuse her, what to teach her and how to enhance the pleasure they both derived from their daily meetings and their frequent correspondence. Her artless, ingenuous affection delighted him as much as his paternal tenderness, his urbanity and his elegance captivated her. At Windsor, when the business of the state was done, he went out riding with her, or watched her playing at battledore and shuttlecock, until with her face flushed, her eyes shining and her small bosom heaving, she reminded him of his lost Caroline, long ago when she was a child at Devonshire House and he in love with her.

Then, at dinner, by the Queen's desire, he sat beside her and was so amusing, she laughed out loud, showing her gums; and although he jibbed a little at first, he soon gave way to her command that the gentlemen should not sit too long a time drinking after the ladies had left the dining-room or, of course, reappear in the drawing-room at all the worse for wear. Court etiquette was strictly observed and conversation between the Queen and her other guests very stilted; but, for the pleasure he had in the Queen's society, Melbourne put up with that too, sitting upright in a little gilt chair until it was time to go to bed, quite forgetting his old easy habits of gambling at White's or lounging about with his feet up on the mantelpiece.

Sometimes the Queen gave a ball at Windsor or Buckingham Palace and no one enjoyed the dancing more in the whirl of brilliant lights and the bejewelled company. Sometimes she went to the opera or the play, and the public received her most warmly. She looked so fresh with her rosy cheeks and her simple, youthful air, and she bore no resemblance whatever to her bankrupt predecessors—to those wicked, self-indulgent uncles of hers with their brandy-coloured faces and their swollen feet, whose eating and drinking and all manner of excess had debauched the royal house of Hanover. 'The Queen,' wrote Melbourne's sister, Lady Cowper, 'is as great a wonder in her way as Fair Star or any other enchanted Princess, and has the good fortune to be peculiarly gifted by the Fairies with *Le don de Plaisir*. What luck it is for this Country to have such a Jewel to raise the Character of Royalty.'

But it was to be a year or two yet before the winds of respectability conducted by this same fairy princess would blow out the last flickering, flamboyant candles of the

Regency. There was still gambling and drinking in St James's, whoring in Covent Garden, eccentricity and extravagance in high society. There was still Holland House, though Lady Holland was getting old and grumpy and more domineering than ever and no one much enjoyed her dinners 'any longer. People went instead—or the young men beginning to make a name in politics and letters did—to Gore House in rural Kensington, where the widowed Lady Blessington, no longer young though still very attractive, sat in a gold-upholstered chair like a throne, with Dickens, Forster, Thackeray, Disraeli and Bulwer-Lytton at her feet and Count d'Orsay hovering about her. Ladies did not go to her salon, for she had never quite succeeded in living down her shady past; and the gentlemen did not take their wives. But no one could be more generous in giving time and sympathy to her friends, even at the cost of destroying her own health. Leisure was something she could not afford at this stage in her career. The Blessington fortune having dwindled away and d'Orsay's extravagance eaten into what remained of it, she was obliged to work far into the night writing fashionable novels and editing *The Book of Beauty*, one of the expensive, glossy annuals covered in watered silk, which at this time, conferred a certain *cachet* on the modish ladies who displayed them in their drawing-rooms as well as providing their idle hours with a little light reading.

D'Orsay, meanwhile, had become the leader of masculine fashion by the 1830s, just as Brummell had been the *arbiter elegantarium* of an earlier decade. Tall and slim with a slender waist and extremely beautiful hands and feet, he was an exquisite creature, with a flood of curly, dark auburn hair and immaculate whiskers; and, unlike Brummell, he was a man of breeding with a cultured mind and an amiable disposition. 'This Phoebus Apollo of dandyism,' Carlyle called him, when he came 'whirling hither in a splendid chariot that struck all Chelsea into mute amazement'; while Jane, highly amused by the sight of this gay humming-bird sitting beside her worthy husband in his grey homespun suit, described the fantastical finery of his dress in more detail: 'Sky-blue satin cravat, yards of gold chain, white French gloves, light drab great-coat lined with velvet of the same colour, invisible inexpressibles, skin-coloured and fitting like a glove.'

Town was d'Orsay's natural habitat and the proper background for his bizarre existence—he had little use for the country. At one time the lover and still the spoilt child of Lady Blessington, he lived in a cottage *ornée* in the grounds of Gore House and at first had no difficulty in leading a life devoted to leisure and pleasure on her hard-won literary earnings and the credit he got from the London shopkeepers. He could have earned his own living as an artist, perhaps—he had talent and was not a fool. Carlyle said he was 'a rather substantial fellow at bottom, by no means without insight'. But this idea of making money out of his drawings only occurred to him once, when his creditors really began to hunt him and he was forced to hide behind the locked gates of Gore House between sunrise and sunset to avoid being served with a summons. Generally he preferred to take a chance in the hope of repairing his fortune at Crockford's, by then the leading gambling club in St James's, and without ever realizing that Crockford himself, who had once been a fishmonger and now sat night after night with his gilded hook baited in the gaming-room, was bound in the end to be the only winner.

Whist and faro had gone out of fashion in favour of the game of hazard which, although illegal, was played by everyone, even bishops and Ministers of the crown; and at Crockford's, where the dinners prepared by Ude, the most famous chef in Europe, were even more *recherchés*

than they had been at Watier's, the high stakes went
even higher as soon as d'Orsay appeared. Since most of
the aristocracy from the Duke of Wellington downwards
belonged to the club, 'the tone was excellent,' Gronow
declared, 'and at the gay and festive board which was
constantly replenished from midnight until early dawn,
the most brilliant sallies of wit, the most agreeable
conversation, the most interesting anecdotes, interspersed with grave political discussions and acute logical
reasoning on every conceivable subject, proceeded from
the soldiers, scholars, statesmen, poets and men of
pleasure who, when "the house was up" and balls and
parties at an end, delighted to finish the evening with a
little supper and a good deal of hazard at old Crockey's.'
Disraeli and Bulwer-Lytton, both young and in love with
dandyism, were often to be seen there, 'displaying at that
brilliant supper table, the one his sable, the other his
auburn curls', and among the Dukes and noble lords
gambling away their inheritance, that staunch Whig,
George Anson, soon to become the trusted friend and
private secretary of the Queen's young husband, Prince
Albert of Saxe-Coburg-Gotha.

According to the Duke of Wellington, it was not the
Queen who was 'a great stickler for morality' at the
beginning of her reign; it was Prince Albert who insisted
on the character of the Court being spotless, 'the Queen
not caring a straw about it', and Prince Albert who was
'extremely strait-laced . . . whereas she was rather the
other way'. The Prince indeed was shocked by Victoria's
headstrong behaviour, her passion for dancing and
playing games; and in spite of the earnest advice he had
received from his uncle, King Leopold, and his tutor,
Baron Stockmar, he was not at all happy at first as the
bridegroom of the Queen of England. 'The difficulty of
filling my place with proper dignity is that I am only the
husband and not the master of the house,' he wrote to his

friend Prince Löwenstein; and it irked him extremely
that Victoria dismissed him from the room when her
Ministers came to see her, refusing to discuss with him
even the most minor affairs of state. She was afraid he
might endeavour to thwart her—and that would spoil
her pleasure in being Queen as well as her delight in being
the wife of someone she already regarded as quite
perfect. For Albert was beautiful in her sight. In her
diary she wrote of 'his beautiful blue eyes and exquisite
nose, and such a pretty mouth with delicate moustaches
and slight, very slight whiskers'—and although she was
determined to get her own way as Queen of England, she
was very much in love with her handsome Prince and
most anxious to prolong the idyllic rapture of their first
few days together at Windsor.

The Prince was patient, tactful and cautious—and in
the first six months of their marriage, very lonely. His
manner in society was formal and very correct; the
English aristocracy did not like it. He was not a fox-
hunting man—he preferred botany; he did not gamble or
eat and drink to excess, or ogle the maids of honour. In
fact he was foreign and therefore un-English and quite
inexplicable; very high-minded and terribly stiff, with
one quite peculiar relaxation that gave him pleasure—he
liked playing the organ. 'How strange he is,' Lady
Lyttelton declared. 'He must have been playing just while
the Queen was finishing her toilette . . . and nobody but
the organ knows what is in him, except indeed, by the
look of his eyes sometimes.'

Strange he remained and a stranger in the land of his
adoption, yet his failure to conquer the aristocracy was
partly due to their insular prejudice and lack of understanding; and before long his success in taming the
Queen far exceeded any disappointment he may have felt
in his awkward relations with society. Within a year the
Queen had almost given up dancing and going to bed in

the early hours of the morning, preferring a simple country life at Windsor or to spend the afternoon at Buckingham Palace listening to Felix Mendelssohn, who came by the Prince's invitation to play his new compositions on the organ and to accompany the Queen when she graciously sang some of his songs. Little by little, with the help of Melbourne and then of Sir Robert Peel, the Prince began to take a share in the Queen's business, and the Queen to trust his judgement and value his advice. By 1842, looking back to the years when she had relied entirely on Lord Melbourne, she wrote in her diary: 'I cannot forbear remarking what an artificial sort of happiness *mine* was *then*, and what a blessing it is I have now in my beloved Husband *real* and solid happiness, which no politics, no worldly reverses *can* change; it could not have lasted long as it was then, for kind and excellent as Lord M. was to me, it was but in society that I had amusement, and I was only living on that superficial resource, which I *then fancied* was happiness. Thank God! for *me* and others, this is changed, and I *know what* REAL happiness is.'

The Prince had won a total victory, and it says much for his integrity that he never sought to abuse the power he had over the Queen of England. Instead he used his influence in public affairs with the utmost discretion, and in his private life with the Queen and their growing family of children set an example of domestic happiness and good behaviour, which had little appeal to the pleasure-loving world of fashion, but was soon to become an established way of life for the rest of the nation. Respectability and royalty had not gone together for such a very long time, the aristocracy could only mock at this new combination; yet the power of the great land-owning families, riddled from within by the extravagance of the Regency and besieged from without by the increasing wealth and importance of the industrial middle classes, was on the decline, and it was among the middle classes that the royal household earned a respect worthy of imitation.

London in the season might still flaunt its gaudy, disreputable features for the raffish sons of the nobility, and the great houses still offer any number of opportunities for gambling and drinking; but when the Queen and her husband went to the opera it was to hear the music of Rossini, Donizetti and Bellini and the inspired singing of Grisi, Mario, Tamburini and Lablache, not to laugh and chatter in their box or to show themselves off, and their serious attitude had a profound effect on the whole musical life of the capital. Audiences began to behave with more dignity and to demand a high standard of performance; foreign musicians, although some of them regarded England as an unmusical country, discovered they could earn larger fees in London than anywhere else in the world. Two Italian opera seasons ran side by side from 1847 to 1852, with Jenny Lind and Henriette Sontag at what was now called Her Majesty's Theatre in the Haymarket, and Grisi, Alboni, Tamburini and Pauline Viardot at Covent Garden, which became known as the Royal Italian Opera House.

Jenny Lind, with a voice of incomparable beauty enhanced by a reputation for the blameless purity of her private life, invoked the adoration of her English audiences, whether at the opera or at the concerts held in the Hanover Square Rooms under the auspices of the Philharmonic Society; and on the new wave of musical appreciation stimulated by the taste of Prince Albert, Mendelssohn, Liszt, Joachim as a boy of thirteen, Berlioz and Wagner were all invited to perform at the Philharmonic Concerts, for which tickets could only be obtained at a premium. Yet for many music-lovers there was no pleasure to be compared with the splendid choral concerts given by the Sacred Harmonic Society at the large Exeter Hall in the Strand, and when Mendelssohn conducted his new oratorio *Elijah* there in the presence of the Queen and the Prince, with a chorus and orchestra of five hundred on the platform, the hall was packed with a crowd of three thousand people listening in rapt silence. Marian Evans, later to become famous as the novelist George Eliot, thought it was 'a glorious production and a kind of sacramental purification of Exeter Hall'; and indeed, the public in general, nurtured on the English tradition of semi-amateur choral singing, felt that oratorios were respectable and could be enjoyed with a good conscience, even though a few dissentient voices were raised on the grounds that the lives of some of the singers 'did not always reflect the sentiments they uttered'.

The theatre continued to be regarded as a far less uplifting form of entertainment, yet even the theatre was becoming less disreputable. There was still Madame Vestris, that dazzling, debonair singing actress of the Regency, whose brilliant comedy and dashing appearance in the breeches parts she played with such abandon, had brightened the theatrical scene for more than twenty years. She no longer ran the little Olympic Theatre which she had made famous with her own startling productions of Planché's *burlettas*, but in 1839 had taken on the management of Covent Garden with her second husband Charles Mathews; a year later, in honour of the Queen's marriage to Prince Albert, staging a tremendous spectacle there, called *The Fortunate Isles*. When the bride and bridegroom came in state to visit this patriotic effusion, Vestris was on her best behaviour; she escorted the royal pair to their box, walking backwards and holding aloft two lighted candelabra. She was forty-three and her superb legs were still the talk of the town, but when she revived *The Beggar's Opera* she wisely dropped the part of Macheath and played Lucy instead. Even Vestris saw the need of becoming more sober.

Edmund Kean had drunk himself to death by 1833 and his son Charles, without the blazing fire of his father's genius and without his tragic weakness, was the Queen's favourite actor. He was such a gentleman and his wife, Ellen Tree, was such a lady—no whiff of scandal ever impaired their reputation; and it was quite within the bounds of propriety to invite them and their company to Windsor at Christmas to play *The Merchant of Venice*. The Queen and her husband felt it was their duty 'to revive and elevate the English drama' and by their patronage, they sought to purge it of its associations with a rowdy, insensitive public. As time went on they arranged for Mr and Mrs Kean to present a number of classical plays in the small theatre Prince Albert had constructed in the Castle and they even encouraged their children, as they grew up, to read and act plays in private.

Privacy as a pleasure was something that royalty had seldom valued before the reign of Queen Victoria. Her exhibitionist uncles had brazened out the scandalous features of their private lives; they had paraded their opulent, overblown mistresses, their debts, their expensive horses and carriages for all the world to see; and Victoria herself had been excited by the splendours of Buckingham Palace when she first moved there from Kensington. But the Prince and her adoration of him had changed all that. He was used to the privacy of his German home, to the tranquillity of the Thuringian Forest and the romantic castle of Rosenau. He taught the Queen to abhor publicity, to retire with him whenever her duty allowed it, into a life of homely simplicity. The economies he made in the management of the royal palaces enabled her to spend about £200,000 on buying Osborne House and its grounds in the Isle of Wight, and here their quiet domesticity was able to flourish 'away from all the bitterness people create for themselves in London' and from 'the inquisitive and often impudent people' who had pestered them when they had visited the Regent's pleasure-dome at Brighton. That exuberant folly of her uncle, the Queen disliked intensely—it was much too gaudy, much too exotic and haunted by ghosts better forgotten; she much preferred her dear Albert's taste, even when it flowered at Osborne House in rows of heavy Germanic busts in bronze set in recesses crowned with gilded plaster shells.

The Prince had his own ideas about art and architecture, and they were curiously mixed. He bought Italian primitives at a time when they were entirely neglected by everyone else—perhaps he saw in them the same high moral purpose he discovered in the more sentimental works of Mr Uwins and the other gentlemen of the Royal Academy to whom he gave encouragement. He liked frescoes if they were large, allegorical, instructive and edifying, and the noble stags Mr Landseer painted against a background of moorland and heather. And his taste in sculpture veered from the pseudo-classical marbles of Thorneycroft and Theed to the reproduction, also in marble, of the hands and feet of his children and the small statuettes he commissioned of the dogs, ponies and Highland gillies attached to the Royal Household.

English architecture did not appeal to the Prince's romantic German taste. He built a Swiss chalet in the garden at Osborne and, some years later, went far more Scottish than any Scotsman had ever thought of going in the new baronial castle he designed at Balmoral, where everything that could be covered in tartan was. There were tartan carpets on the floors, tartan chair-covers, tartan linoleums, and curtains with frills of the Balmoral tartan in red and grey, the Victoria tartan with a white stripe and the Royal Stuart tartan of the Queen's distant forbears. She thought it was all utterly *beautiful*. 'Every year,' she wrote, 'my heart becomes more fixed in this dear paradise, and so much more so now, that *all* has become my dear Albert's *own* creation, own work, own building . . . and his great taste, and the impress of his dear hand have been stamped everywhere.' And the effect of the Highlands on Albert's sometimes melancholy spirits sent her into raptures of delight also. 'It is a happiness to see him!' she exclaimed. 'Oh! What can equal the beauties of nature! What enjoyment there is in them! Albert enjoys it so much; he is in ecstasies here!'

What with the bag-pipes, the pony rides, the sketching-parties and the picnics, the highland games and the highland people, the mountains and the cairns and the red deer, the braes and the brooks and the heather, and pretending on their expeditions in the country to be Lord and Lady This or That instead of themselves, life was so *gemütlich*, the Queen was as happy as the day is long with her adored Albert. Together they shared the enjoyment of a simple holiday with only the sky and the rain and the mist to watch them and at last some leisure from the cares of state, the harassing business and pomp of royalty.

But it was a new kind of pleasure, removed from the self-indulgent and shameless behaviour of the previous generation, and one which marked a fundamental change of outlook. With the high-minded example of industry and prudence set by the Queen and Prince Albert, the puritan instinct lying dormant in the English people was reawakened. Life was no longer an extravagant joke devoted to the uninhibited gratification of the senses. Life was serious, life was a discipline. Duty predominated and pleasure was permissible only if it went hand in hand with decorum.

6

HOLIDAYS

and

EXCURSIONS

THE NEW TREND towards piety and decorum in the early years of Queen Victoria's reign belonged to a period of almost unprecedented social and economic change in Britain. Between the first Reform Bill of 1832 and the second, passed in 1867, the division between the old easy-going way of life in the rural districts and the new way of life in the industrial towns of the upstart manufacturers became more distinct. Gradually the towns were beginning to encroach on the countryside and to dominate the lives of a far larger section of the people than ever before. The urban middle classes, ever increasing in number, now had more power in the government of the nation, more wealth from the new industrial techniques they themselves had invented, and a strong bias towards the more rabid Evangelical and Nonconformist movements in religion. They eyed the privileged excesses of the aristocracy with a severe, half-envious disapprobation, at the same time failing almost entirely to perceive their own errors in grinding down the people who worked for them.

Not all the industrialists were villains. By the 1820s Sir Robert Peel, father of the great statesman, and Robert Owen the mill-owner of Lanark, had already begun to agitate for state control of the appalling conditions in the factories, where children of eight or nine years old worked a sixteen-hour day; nevertheless the number of employers who held family prayers in the dining-room before setting out for their factories after a very large breakfast, and were able to view the half-starved children they employed there with perfect equanimity, was considerable. They did not, of course, believe in leisure or pleasure for the masses; they believed that God had called them into that station of life where obedience and meekness were all. Leisure for the lower orders signified drunkenness, sabotage and riot. While the good among them could go to Chapel on Sundays to be saved, the bad must suffer for their sins; it all fitted in very neatly with what was written in the Bible.

What is more it fitted in with the example set by the royal family. No one could be kinder or more condescending than Queen Victoria when she stopped her carriage in the wilds of Scotland to give a warm petticoat to the old crofter's widow living in a hut on the mountain-side; no one took more pleasure in helping the deserving poor. But 'deserving' was the operative word on the Victorian conscience, and the beef and ale and the merry-making liberally dispensed by the aristocracy in the countryside were unknown to the unfortunate dwellers in the urban slums; they apparently deserved nothing, not even the decencies of life. Yet a man could, by sheer persistence and rugged force of character, rise from the lower strata into the more salubrious air of gentility enjoyed by the middle classes, if he had a gift for engineering and was not afraid of experiment. The new machinery in the noisy, smoky industrial towns was hungry for men with expert knowledge. Diligence, inventiveness, hard work and thrift paid off as never before or since, and the driving force of individual enterprise was worshipped with the same assiduous attention as the word of God. To many people the powerful new developments in engineering represented the highest progress yet achieved by mankind.

No single event in the nineteenth century so changed the face of England and the social habits of the nation as the development of the railways. Whole towns and villages on what had been the great coaching routes throughout the country, with their posting-inns and the good food and wine to be had in them, began to fall into decay as travellers forsook the roads for the railways. Travelling by coach had always been expensive for the middle classes, a luxury few of them could afford; travelling by rail was much cheaper, besides being a novel experience and so fast it appealed to everyone in search of adventure. Even those like Charles Greville, who could afford to go by coach, enjoyed the new mode of travelling for the fun of it. 'The first sensation is a slight degree of nervousness and of being run away with,' he wrote of his trip to Liverpool, 'but a sense of security soon supervenes, and the velocity is delightful. Town after town, one park and *château* after another, are left behind with the rapid variety of a moving panorama, and the continual bustle and animation of the changes and stoppages make the journey very entertaining.'

Not everyone, however, was quite so enthusiastic as the Clerk to the Privy Council. Prince Albert was alarmed by the speed of the first rail journey he took and begged the conductor of the train 'not to go so fast next time'. Some people were frightened of being crushed to pieces in the dark tunnels or shaken out of the carriages as they sped across viaducts and rattled downhill at a terrifying pace. Others, if they belonged to the nobility, had their own carriages strapped to the rolling-stock because it was beneath their dignity to be seen travelling with the *hoi polloi*, while some refused to travel by rail at all and objected very strongly to the desecration of the countryside. Lady Hastings complained that one of the proposed new lines would be visible from her windows and George Grote, the Radical Member of Parliament, was disgusted by what he called 'this age of steam and cant'. Yet, before long most of the public had come to agree with Sydney Smith, who declared: 'Railroad travelling is a delightful improvement of human life. Man is become a bird; he can fly longer and quicker than a Solan goose. . . . Everything is near, everything is immediate—time, distance and delay are abolished.' And indeed, the new railway system which spread its tentacles so rapidly and irrevocably throughout the length and breadth of Britain in the first great railway boom in the 1840s, made long distance travelling a pleasure to a great number of people who had never thought of going on a journey before.

Even the Highlands of Scotland became accessible to a new class of traveller, for until now only the wealthy tourists, inspired by *The Lady of the Lake* and the Waverley novels of Sir Walter Scott, had been able to travel so far by post-chaise or private carriage, to explore the romantic scenery of the Trossachs and Loch Katrine so brilliantly described by the 'Wizard of the North'. The great man himself, at home among the shields and weapons and trophies hung on the walls at Abbotsford, the vast baronial castle designed for him by Edward Blore in the new style of 'Castle Gothic' that was to become so popular as the century went on, was also the object of their pilgrimage. He entertained his friends and admirers with a princely hospitality and suffered a good

deal from intruders even then; but before his prophecy
that the increasing power of steam would 'waft friends
in the course of a few hours' from London to the banks
of the Tweed had come true, he was a dying man.

Had he lived a few years longer, no doubt he would
have shared the sentiments of Wordsworth, that other
great peak of the Romantic Revival in literature, who
lived on for another twenty years at Rydal Mount to be
pestered by sightseers arriving in the Lake District, guide-
book in hand, to seek out the setting of his poems and to
force their way into his garden in the hope of accosting
him as he took the evening air. According to Harriet
Martineau in one of her more acid moments, he very
much enjoyed the adulation he received and did not
object at all to putting himself on show to the summer
visitors; but he did object very strongly to the proposed
extension of the railway from Kendal to Windermere. 'A
vivid perception of romantic scenery is neither inherent
in mankind nor a necessary consequence of even a com-
prehensive education', he wrote. 'Rocks and mountains,
torrents and wide spread waters . . . cannot in their finer
relations to the human mind, be comprehended without
opportunities of culture in some degree habitual.' It was
therefore of no benefit to anyone to bring hordes of
excursionists by rail from the Black Country to Grasmere.
'Persons in that condition, when upon holiday, or on a
Sunday, after having attended divine worship,' would be
better off, he thought, making 'little excursions with their
wives and children among the neighbouring fields within
reach of their own urban dwellings', instead of invading
the lakeside country and upsetting the peace of its
inhabitants with their loud and vulgar behaviour. This
view did not quite tally with the poet's earlier belief in
the liberty of the human spirit, but Wordsworth was old
now and it was natural that he should want to defend the
country he had loved so dearly all his life, besides

considering himself to be an authority on what was fit for it and what was not.

He held strong views on the architecture that was suitable for the romantic scenery of Westmorland, objecting to the 'baldness' of the Georgian style and welcoming with pleasure the new combination of Castle Gothic and Church Gothic with its mullioned windows, ornamental chimneys and fretted roof-lines, designed to imitate the picturesque cottages and houses of an earlier age. If he ever saw it, he probably approved of Richard Brown's book on *Domestic Architecture* which appeared in 1841. This attempted to satisfy the nineteenth-century mania for building and adapting to the English scene anything from the past that was considered worthy of resuscitation. It offered an immense variety of styles from the cottage *ornée* to the baronial castle, with the Pompeian suburban villa, the Egyptian pavilion or the mock-Tudor gabled mansion in between, and suggested the correct setting of woodland, park or mountain-side for each style. Industrialism disguised as art, was, in fact, vitiating the taste of those who could afford to build new houses and Georgian elegance in retreat.

Harriet Martineau, on her first visit to Westmorland in 1845, took such delight in 'the amethyst mountains at sunset and the groves and white beaches beside the lake', she decided to build a house at Ambleside where she could relax from the hectic life she led in London as a successful writer of political propaganda and the most famous lioness yet to appear on the literary scene. Wordsworth told her that her decision to build 'The Knoll' was a wise one, giving her a good deal of gratuitous advice, which she complacently ignored or perhaps did not hear through her ear-trumpet. But she invited him to plant a tree in the garden and was soon enjoying the parties and picnics on the Lakes she organized for her literary friends and exploring the mountains in a gig or on foot, 'wit and repartee genially flowing the while'. Thorough in all things, she eventually wrote *A Guide to the Lakes* for the benefit of the visitors who came on the new railway Wordsworth had not been able to stop, though their effrontery caused her great pain. The most vulgar of them waylaid her in the garden, stole her flowers and came right up to 'The Knoll' to stare in at the windows, so that she must have wondered sometimes if the railway really was quite the blessing she had always hoped it would be, even though it served the common people whose cause she had always supported with so much energy.

One young friend of hers, James Payne, described the 'fever' of the summer months at Ambleside. 'Our inns are filled to bursting,' he declared, 'our private houses broken into by parties desperate for lodgings. . . . A great steam monster ploughs up our lake and disgorges multitudes upon the pier; the excursion trains bring thousands of curious, vulgar people, who mistake us for the authoress next door, and compel us to forge her autograph; the donkeys in our streets increase and multiply a hundredfold, tottering under the weight of enormous females visiting our water-falls from morn to eve; we are ruthlessly eyed by painters and brought into foregrounds and backgrounds as "warm tints" or "bits of repose"; our hills are darkened by swarms of tourists; our lawns are picnicked upon by twenty at a time, and our trees branded with initial letters. . . . '

What Wordsworth had feared had actually happened— pleasure for the masses had been made possible by the arrival of the railway and the new kind of tourist did not know how to behave. 'The stranger must spend a day in the mountains—if alone, so much the better,' Miss Martineau wrote in her *Guide*, without suggesting how he was to get away from his fellow trippers. Perhaps she noticed what she was the first to call 'the tourist season' less as she grew older. She had already suffered one serious illness which had been cured by mesmerism, and at the age of fifty she retired to 'The Knoll' and took to her bed believing her end was near, though in fact she lived for another twenty years on a diet of oysters, turtle soup and brandy, continuing to write as many as six leading articles a week for the *Daily News*, while enjoying the boxes of cigars sent to her by the editor.

And there was no stopping the movement she had done so much to foster by her pen. The working classes had begun to realize that they, as well as the rest of the nation, were entitled to some leisure and pleasure, provided the diversion they sought did not conflict with their general belief in the virtue of hard work. Thomas Cook, a Baptist missionary and one of Father Mathew's temperance converts, was their best friend, for it was he who arranged the first excursion train from Leicester to Loughborough to encourage those who could not afford more than a shilling to attend a temperance meeting in Loughborough. Four years later, in 1845, he conducted his first pleasure trip from Leicester to Liverpool, travelling personally with the train and charging 14s for the first-class passengers and 10s for the second class. Ticket-holders were warned to be up early as the train was due to leave Leicester at five o'clock in the morning; accommodation at the hotels in Liverpool would be found for them, and Cook published a small guide-book on the places of interest not to be missed. So many people wished to avail themselves of this unique opportunity, there was almost a riot at the railway station and Thomas Cook was satisfied that his philanthropic idea of improving the minds of ordinary folk by means of cheap travel could be turned into a commercial success. Before long his name was to become famous and his organization to extend far and wide beyond the shores of England, bringing foreign travel within the means of men in boots and bowler hats and women who had never dared to cross the Channel.

At home, the railways immediately opened up the seaside to a great number of people who had never seen the sea before. Charlotte Brontë went to Bridlington in 1839 full of anticipation. 'The idea of seeing the SEA—of being near it—watching its changes by sunrise, sunset—moonlight—and noonday—in calm—perhaps in storm—fills and satisfies my mind,' she wrote—and she was not disappointed; indeed she was so overwhelmed by the sight of it, she burst into tears and even when she had made 'the sternest efforts' to subdue her emotions, was 'very quiet and subdued for the remainder of the day'. The more frivolous aspects of the seaside did not appeal to her at all. She viewed the evening parade on the pier as 'the greatest absurdity', for the visitors assembled there in such numbers, their only amusement was 'to march round and round in regular file to secure any movement whatever'.

Not that Bridlington was ever so crowded as some of the other resorts. Brighton, with its proximity to London and the number of stage coaches that went there daily, had already lost much of its exclusiveness by the time the railway opened in 1841. The first excursion train three years later was so popular, it started from London Bridge at half-past eight in the morning with forty-five carriages and four engines, went on to New Cross where six more carriages and a fifth engine had to be added, and at Croydon took on another six carriages and yet another engine. By one o'clock this fantastic steam caterpillar had not reached Brighton and a director of the railway company went up the line in a pilot engine to look for it; but the passengers, who numbered close on two thousand, were delighted with their journey and half the townsfolk of Brighton turned out to welcome them. Murmurings from the more aristocratic residents about 'those swarms . . . daily and weekly disgorged on the Steyne from the cancer-like arms of the railroad' were of no avail. Brighton was popular with every class of person in search of fun and its shrimps appealed as much to Disraeli who stayed there in 1840 as to the Cockney crowds who came for the day.

No one enjoyed it more than Thackeray, who called it 'London *plus* prawns for breakfast and the sea air'. It amused him to watch the people on the crowded Steyne: the railroad directors, nabobs, barristers and famous actors and actresses down from London; and the tight-laced dragoons, 'trotting up and down with solemn, handsome, stupid faces and huge yellow moustachios', who wove their way among 'the cabs, the flys, the shandry-dans, the sedan-chairs with the poor invalids inside, the old maids' and the dowagers' chariots, and the hacks mounted by young ladies from the equestrian schools.' On the beach there were donkeys, ponies and dogs; little boys with spades and shrimping nets; young ladies with novels and young gentlemen with dandified canes; mamas with their babies, their sewing and their sunshades, and papas with *The Times* and their telescopes, their tall hats and their tobacco. Bottles of tea, of beer and ginger pop, hampers of buns, meat-pies and pasties were strewn around them, and the noise was continuous from the shouting, giggling, squalling multitude and the bright brass instruments of the German bands. Dickens commented on the noise of the innumerable itinerant musicians at Broadstairs with their 'most excruciating' organs, fiddles, bells and music-boxes in full blast under his window; and Jane Carlyle, a few years later when the Nigger Minstrels had arrived, wrote from Ramsgate: 'A brass band plays all through our breakfast and repeats the performance often during the day, and is succeeded by a band of Ethiopians, and that again by a band of female fiddlers! and interspersed with these are individual barrel-organs, individual Scotch bagpipes and individual French horns!'—a veritable orgy of sound to add to the frolic and the fun.

But bathing was still a serious business—'a luxury to the healthful and a restorative to the sick'. Doctors were still recommending the drinking of sea water 'mixed with port wine, milk or beef tea to make it more palatable'. In cases of languor, debility, hysterical affections, St Vitus's Dance, scrofula, rickets, measles and whooping cough, however, they prescribed a plunge into the cold ocean, often at the break of day when their unhappy victims could not so easily be spied upon. Mixed bathing was strictly forbidden, since the gentlemen went in naked, and it was considered a great stain on the gentility of Brighton that the bathing machines there were not fitted with a 'modesty hood', the invention of a Margate Quaker named Benjamin Beale. Without this enormous striped umbrella, which could be unfurled at the back of the machine after it had been drawn into the water by a lumbering horse and reversed, the gentlemen as they stood shivering on the steps were naturally wholly exposed as nature made them to anyone sitting on the cliffs with a telescope. The spectators who found it shocking, could, of course, have put their telescopes down or have looked the other way, but they seldom did. Some ladies rather enjoyed themselves as self-appointed watch-dogs, deliberately sitting on the beach in the bathing area and spoiling the pleasure of the embarrassed gentlemen.

None of the ladies themselves when they bathed could have been accused of immodesty. They were protected by a thick flannel cloak tied with a string round the neck, or they donned a dark blue bathing-dress fastened with strings round the ankles—and thus encumbered were forcibly put under the water by the lusty male or female dippers attending the machines. Very little pleasure can have been derived from the whole operation, whether in sickness or in health, and very little amusement granted to the onlookers hoping to see a little more than the top of their damp heads. But it was not until the 1860s that a more enlightened attitude to bathing was proposed by a certain Dr Spencer Thomson, who was very much against the idea of forcing people into the water against their will. 'A good many take this step because they think it a duty if they go to the seaside,' he wrote, 'and a good many think they enjoy it or ought to enjoy it because they see others doing so, and yet they have a very gasping pleasure after all.'

Fortunately there were other attractions at the seaside for those who genuinely disliked Dr Thomson's 'gasping pleasure'. There were the libraries, with various rooms where lectures and scientific demonstrations were sometimes given, and where 'young ladies in maroon-coloured gowns and black velvet bracelets' presided over the very mild games of chance or dispensed the fancy articles for sale in the miniature shops. The better class visitors of the gentle sex forgathered there to show off their newest gowns, to gossip and drink sherbert, or to borrow the latest novels and buy souvenirs, knick-knacks, sweet-meats and stationery, while the gallant young gentlemen, who likewise appeared there if they could find no other amusement, came for the purpose of quizzing the young ladies. On wet days the libraries were crowded; on fine days, looking for shells and seaweed to take home and preserve amused the visitors, or they enjoyed strolling on the pier with the delicious sensation at high tide of walking on the water, and at night, the thousand and one little coloured lights competing with the stars in the sky.

At Margate and at Brighton the theatres flourished, with 'blazing Macreadys, resplendent Miss Cushmans, fiery Wallacks, and the like', travelling down from

London to act during the season. And at Broadstairs, which was Dickens's favourite resort, the Tivoli Gardens were a kind of miniature Vauxhall, where concerts were given in the evenings and people danced in the open air. Dickens danced there with his sister-in-law Georgina Hogarth—his wife was expecting a baby; and flirted with another young lady, almost drowning her in one of his most exuberant moods off the end of the pier. 'We enjoy this place amazingly,' he wrote to Forster—and no wonder, for besides the dancing and the flirting, the silly games of Animal, Vegetable and Mineral and the charades they got up with Dickens himself playing King Louis of France in a wide-brimmed hat pinned up at the side with a large feather, there were trips to Pegwell Bay in a hired landau, walks along the beach to Ramsgate and gay adventures in the boats they hired to go sailing out to sea.

Broadstairs was popular with a number of Dickens's friends—old Samuel Rogers, the Macreadys, the Sala family and the Smithsons among them; and the lodgings there were better than in some of the other resorts. Marian Evans spent a month in 'the snuggest little lodging conceivable with a motherly good woman and a nice little damsel of fourteen' to wait on her, all for a guinea a week. She went into raptures over the tranquil evening skies and the glorious colours of the sea and wrote that Broadstairs was perfect, but warned her friends against Ramsgate, which she called 'a strip of London come out for an airing'. With her highly introverted nature and her lack of humour, she never realized that to some people crowds could be fun, the noise and the bustle and the vulgar pushing and shoving adding much to their pleasure in a day by the sea.

Jane Carlyle did not think much of Ramsgate either—the smells were bad; and wherever she went she always seemed to be very unfortunate in her choice of lodgings. At Ryde in 1843, after what she described as a very unpleasant journey in a 'particularly shaky' railway carriage, she found the chief hotel 'the dearest in Europe' and the most uncomfortable she had ever visited. 'The cream was blue milk, the butter tasted of straw and the "cold fowl" was a *lukewarm* one and as tough as leather.' After a sleepless night, 'fevered and nervous from her journey' and worried by the insistent barking of all the dogs in the neighbourhood, she moved to what she hoped would be a quieter lodging, only to be badly bitten by bugs all through the next night. Not surprisingly she fled back to Chelsea, declaring that the only pleasure in taking a holiday was to be found in the bliss of returning home. 'I have not for a long time enjoyed a more triumphant moment than in descending from the railway yesterday at Vauxhall,' she wrote to her husband. 'To be sure I looked (and felt) as if just returning from the Thirty-Years War. Sleepless, bug-bitten, bedusted and bedevilled, I was hardly recognizable . . . but still I was returning with my shield, not on it. A few minutes more, and I should be purified to the shift, to the very skin—should have absolutely bathed myself with eau-de-Cologne—should have some mutton broth set before me and a silver spoon to eat it with (these four days had taught me to appreciate my luxuries), and prospect of my own red bed at night! That of itself,' she concluded joyfully, 'was enough to make me the most thankful woman in Chelsea!'

7

'MYRIADS
of
WONDERFUL
THINGS'

THE RAILWAYS, BOTH as a means of travel and of transport for the heavy goods manufactured in the North and the Midlands, made a vital contribution to the outstanding success of Prince Albert's most brilliant achievement—the setting up of the Great Exhibition of 1851, which gave pleasure to more than six million people.

From the very beginning the Prince and his close associate Henry Cole were inspired by an idealistic enthusiasm for their ambitious project. This was to be a Peace Festival, uniting the industry and art of all the nations of the earth, for as the Prince wrote in the catalogue: 'The progress of the human race resulting from the labour of all men ought to be the final object of the exertion of each individual. In promoting this end we are carrying out the will of the great and blessed God.' Unfortunately *The Times* and Colonel Sibthorp, the Member of Parliament for Lincoln, did not share the visionary conception of the Prince. 'By a stroke of the pen,' *The Times* declared, 'our pleasant Park—nearly the only spot where Londoners can get a breath of fresh air—is to be turned into something between Wolverhampton and Greenwich Fair. The project looks so like insanity that . . . we can scarcely bring ourselves to believe that the advisers of the Prince have dared to connect his name with such an outrage to the feelings and wishes of the inhabitants of the metropolis.' And Colonel Sibthorp went even further. 'As for the object for which Hyde Park is to be desecrated, it is the greatest trash, the greatest fraud and the greatest imposition ever to be palmed upon the people of this country,' he cried, adding that every species of fraud and immorality would be practised by the bad characters attracted to the Exhibition and that people living in the neighbourhood would be wise 'to keep a sharp look out for their silver forks and spoons and servant maids'.

None the less the Prince and his commissioners held steadily to their purpose, and after some hesitation, accepted Joseph Paxton's superbly original design of the Crystal Palace, which met one of Colonel Sibthorp's less serious objections by enclosing the large elm trees growing on the site within the great arched roof of the North Transept instead of cutting them down. The entire output of the nation was used to provide the 293,655 panes of glass needed to furnish the building, which covered some nineteen acres of ground and was three times the size of St Paul's; and when it was finished it presented a dazzling spectacle on the eye, exciting the utmost wonder and delight, and in Queen Victoria a constant surprise, because, as she kept on reminding everyone, Paxton was 'only a gardener's boy' who had risen 'from the lowest grade of society to the highest by his own merits'.

On the opening day, 1 May, Green Park and Hyde Park were 'one mass of densely crowded human beings, in the highest good humour and most enthusiastic'. Some had camped out all night in their carriages, being unable to find accommodation with friends or relations, and their footmen were serving them with breakfast. Less well-to-do people were munching pies and biscuits after sleeping in the Park or on the pavements. A light shower did not worry them at all; soon the sun was shining and the Queen in pink and silver with a diamond ray diadem in her hair and more diamonds on her bosom, was driving by in state with her beloved husband and her two eldest children. The crowd cheered, the pomp and the pageantry a free entertainment worth coming miles to see, yet the Queen and her family so like themselves really in the enjoyment of her domestic happiness. Only ticket-holders, of course, were allowed inside the Crystal Palace. Thackeray, by then as Charlotte Brontë somewhat spitefully noted 'the pet and darling of high society', was one of them; and although he pretended not to be very interested in the Exhibition itself, he said: 'It was a noble awful great love inspiring goose flesh bringing sight . . . the general effect, the multitude, the riches, the peace, the splendour, the security, the sunshine great to see—much grander than a coronation—the vastest and sublimest popular festival that the world has ever witnessed.'

For the Queen it was the happiest day of her life. 'The tremendous cheering, the joy expressed in every face, the vastness of the building, with all its decorations and exhibits, the sound of the organ (with 200 instruments and 600 voices, which seemed nothing) and my beloved husband, the creator of this festival "uniting the industry and art of all the nations of the earth", all this was indeed moving and a day to live for ever,' she wrote. 'God bless my dearest Albert and my dear Country, which has shown itself so great today.' The nave was full of people, every face was bright and smiling; the old Duke of Wellington walked arm in arm with Lord Anglesey—'a touching sight'; the Archbishop blessed the proceedings; Mr Paxton looked truly happy—and no wonder since he *was* only a gardener's boy; the crystal fountain glittered and the absurd reports of dangers of every kind and sort put out by a set of people—'the *soi-disant* fashionables' who still disliked Prince Albert—were silenced. Dearest Albert's name was immortalized for ever. Even *The Times* came round and was reminded of 'that solemn day when all ages and climes shall be gathered round the Throne of their Maker'.

Nothing had ever excited or pleased the Queen quite so much. She went two or three times a week to the Exhibition, until she was 'quite beaten . . . her head bewildered from the beautiful and wonderful things'. It was all *so* beautiful and she praised *everything*—from the stuffed elephant in the Indian section to the chair made from a lump of English coal and the model indoor fountain in the Asiatic style which could be conveniently converted in winter into a fireplace. The outsize marble Amazon being attacked by a ferocious lion thrilled her; the inlaid pianos, the maps on gutta-percha, the Gothic armchairs, the papier mâché and mother-of-pearl paper-racks, fans and work-boxes vied for her admiration with the carved sheepskin picture frames, the chenille carpets, the paisley shawls and the porcelain portraits of herself and her beloved Albert. How *wonderful* it all was—with above all the comfortable, happy feeling, the proud assurance from all this evidence, that British industry was second to none among the other nations of the world.

Visitors poured into the Crystal Palace, not all of them quite so uncritical as the Queen. 'I find I am "used up"

by the Exhibition,' Dickens wrote. 'I don't say there is
nothing in it: there's too much. I have only been twice,
so many things bewilder one. I have a natural horror of
sights, and the fusion of so many sights in one, has not
decreased it. I am not sure that I have seen anything but
the Fountain and the Amazon.' Jane Carlyle also found it
exhausting. The fatigue of even the most cursory survey
was 'indescribable' and the Hope diamond very disappointing— it looked like a lump of crystal, which she
compared in size and shape to a thumb joint; and
although the North Transept was 'rather imposing for
a few minutes', there was nothing really worth looking at
—or nothing that could not be seen in the shops.

But whatever the more sophisticated visitors thought
of the Exhibition, to those who came up from the country
and the provincial towns, the Crystal Palace was a sight
never to be forgotten. While Colonel Sibthorp went on
raving about the demoralization of the people and the
way the poor were being 'seduced' to part with their
savings or pawn their belongings to pay for their journey
to the metropolis, the people themselves in remote towns
and villages all over the country were banding together
in clubs and groups to take advantage of the cheap
excursion trains under the guidance of Thomas Cook, or,
as the catalogue recommended, of some leader, 'if a little
higher in station or influence than the rest so much the
better'. They came in hundreds and in thousands: clergy-
men and their parishioners; workers from the mines, the
shipyards and the cotton mills; yokels from Sussex and
Surrey in their smock frocks and round hats; boys and
girls in button boots and thick clothing. They came to
stare and to gape, their pleasure in no way diminished by
their aching feet and their proximity to each other in the
hot, overcrowded building. They got very tired and very
thirsty and, like their Queen, quite bewildered by so many
wonderful things. But for a shilling at the gate they could

spend the whole day roaming round the Exhibition, and they had never seen anything like it before.

Very early in the proceedings the Prince had decided to forbid the sale of alcohol in the restaurants: glasses of filtered water were provided free instead; and the public bought over 1,000,000 bottles of lemonade, more than 900,000 Bath buns and a similar number of plain buns to consume on the premises. The coffee, according to one visitor, was 'nearly cold and good for nothing', the sandwiches were very expensive and very dry and 'the little dry, sixpenny dollops of pork pie' most unsatisfying. No one, however, could become obstreperous on cold coffee, lemonade and filtered water, and in consequence it was observed that the industrial classes behaved with the utmost decorum. They were seen to be 'well-dressed, orderly and sedate, engaged in examining all that interests them, not quarrelsome or obstinate, but playing with manifest propriety and good temper the important part assigned to them at this gathering of the nations.'

Most of them had never been to London before; most of them had never seen anything like the marble Amazon or the countless other objects on view. And some of them returned home with new ideas and new ambitions, caught up in the ceaseless, respectable endeavour of improving themselves and their surroundings, which meant aping their betters with more comfort in their homes, more ease, more luxury, more leisure. Why should they not aspire to an upright piano or a harp in the parlour, to an ornamental lamp holder with the figure of Asia crowning Britannia? Why not a fringed Indian cloth for the mantelpiece, a bamboo chair with chintz cushions, a japanned coal-box with Landseer's *Dignity and Impudence* on the lid? Why not a tête-à-tête or a back-to-back horsehair sofa, or a fire-screen showing Faith, Hope and Charity encircled in pale convolvulus worked in wool or mother-of-pearl? Why not, indeed? They worked hard, they were making money; they felt they were entitled to spend it wisely on filling their homes with agreeable ornaments. Never had Britain been more prosperous, never had God and Mammon concurred so well. In countless Nonconformist chapels on Sundays, in the Anglican churches and at family prayers in the dining-room, the upper and the lower middle classes felt worthy of the comforts they were earning in this world and of the reward their virtue would surely obtain in the next. God was on their side.

And servants were still cheap and plentiful. They were also a status symbol. To keep a carriage and a manservant gave the household an upper-class air of richness and prosperity denied to those who hired a carriage and employed a female staff; though a house with a head parlour-maid, a cook at £20 a year and one or two house-maids or 'tweeny' maids could boast of the required standard of gentility which most people of the middle classes were content to enjoy. Below this it was at least necessary to employ 'a girl' of sorts, not to be something of a pariah socially or to fall into the class of genteel poverty, where life was hard indeed and appearances had to be kept up at all costs above the invisible line drawn between the polite world and the jungle of the lower orders.

Servants guaranteed the leisure of their employers, yet the mistress of the house with a large family was by no means idle. She felt it was her duty to look after them well and to see that nothing was wasted. Store-cupboards and linen-cupboards had to be kept locked; young children, unless there was a governess in the house, given their lessons; the cook encouraged to make marmalade, jam, pickled walnuts and ginger preserves. Potted plants, nursed up in the conservatory at the right temperature and with infinite care, had to be watered, and long letters written to innumerable friends and relations to keep them *au courant* with the family news. The ritual of calling and leaving cards had to be meticulously observed and was quite an occupation in itself, since a knowledge of this most intricate maze of etiquette was a mark of good breeding and one which separated the sheep from the goats in a decisive manner.

The ritual of giving a dinner party was equally complex. Invitations went out at least a month before the date and the cook was given her orders well in advance. Guests were paired off according to rank and precedence, the host leading the procession into the dining-room with the highest ranking lady on his arm. The meal was long and elaborate, beginning with the soup, the fish and the 'removes' or side dishes, and going on to the serious business of the entrées and the roasts into the sweets and savouries and finally the dessert of fruit and nuts, bonbons and sweetmeats, to the moment when the hostess 'collected eyes' to signal that it was time for the ladies to rise and leave the room. Formality and the need to reciprocate after being entertained ruled the choice of guests, though at Oxford where this convention was strictly observed among the heads of the colleges, it did not always give pleasure. 'In the case of the Blisses at Corpus,' wrote Mrs Jeune, the wife of the Master of Pembroke, 'it is *we* not *they* who have appeared to drop the acquaintance by not inviting them in turn, and now it is too late to mend the matter. Mrs Bliss, I know is extremely punctilious about returning dinner for dinner, so I suppose we may consider them quite struck off our visiting list. The loss,' she added, rather acidly, 'is not very great.'

And indeed dinner parties were often given more for the pleasure of showing off a good table than for the entertainment of the guests who were invited. Kate Dickens, being young and inexperienced when she moved with her husband to Devonshire Terrace, rather

overdid the decorations to her table with quantities of
artificial flowers: 'The very candles rose out of an artificial rose,' according to Jane Carlyle, 'and the profusion
of figs, raisins and oranges absolutely overloaded the
dessert.' Dickens, however, was a charming host, having
learnt the art of giving pleasure to his guests in the salon
of Lady Blessington. He was besides 'a highflyer at
fashion' and indulged in fancy waistcoats, brightly
coloured neckcloths and jewelled pins, which added
greatly to his fascination and the striking character of
his appearance. After dinner at home he frequently
entertained the company with readings from his own
work or, to satisfy his overwhelming passion for acting,
got up elaborate amateur theatricals; and he was equally
good at amusing his own or Macready's young children
with his brilliant feats as a conjuror. 'Only think of that
excellent Dickens playing the *conjuror* for one whole
hour—and the best conjuror I ever saw!' Jane Carlyle
exclaimed. 'The entertainment concluded with a plum
pudding made out of raw flour, raw eggs—all the usual
raw ingredients—boiled in a gentleman's hat—and
tumbled out reeking—all in one minute before the eyes
of the astonished children and astonished grown people!'

Dickens was fully aware of his own power to astonish
everyone. The more successful he became the more he
was invited out, the number of his friends increasing
with his fame as a writer. At his 'book dinners' at the
Star and Garter at Richmond, Maclise and Macready,
Landseer, Stanfield, Marryat and Forster all contributed
to the brilliant conversation and the wit of the convivial
occasion while Dickens himself glowed with pleasure and
satisfaction. But great men did not always make dinner
parties amusing. Mrs Jeune went to one in honour of Mr
Gladstone and found it extremely dull because all the
other gentlemen at the table were so absorbed in listening
to him, they took no notice of the ladies sitting next to

them. Mrs Gladstone also behaved rather strangely; she disappeared when the ladies rose from the table and did not return to the drawing-room until the gentlemen came upstairs, evidently preferring their company to that of her own sex. It was sometimes at this crucial moment, especially if the gentlemen sat too long over their port, that the hostess ran out of small talk and fell into despair about the way her party was going; even Mrs Jeune was not always successful in bridging the gap between the serious business of eating and the more irritable process of digestion afterwards. She was happier when entertaining the undergraduates from her husband's college or chaperoning 'a string of young ladies' to the balls and parties in Commemoration Week, and when Dr Jeune was made Vice-Chancellor, she started giving a reception every Friday evening, which added greatly to the social gaiety of Oxford.

Mrs Jeune's 'string of young ladies' in Oxford probably had more opportunities of enjoying themselves than the girls who grew up in less intellectual surroundings. As children they had plenty of freedom and of fun among their brothers and sisters and numerous cousins, some families being so large and closely knit there was no need for them to know anyone outside their own circle. They had parlour games and picnics and boating-parties, with aunts and uncles and older cousins and perhaps an indulgent grandmother to watch over their childish romps. But once a girl had left the schoolroom behind, her freedom vanished. She became a young lady, bound by a code of behaviour as tight as the stays she was compelled to wear and as stuffy as the innumerable petticoats she put on to stiffen her crinoline skirt. With her hair in ringlets and her feet in dainty slippers, her waist pulled in and her skirt on the ground, her physical movements were closely restricted. She might enjoy a game of croquet, where the starchy eye of the chaperon could sometimes be dodged and a word or two whispered in confidence between the sexes; otherwise all opportunities of talking to a young man without the constant supervision of an older relation were hard to come by. And although young ladies everywhere had leisure enough—more than they knew what to do with—their occupations did not fill their minds, yearning wistfully beneath the taboos of a society growing ever more strict and conventional.

Their object was to find a husband and their appeal to the opposite sex was judged by their seeming air of innocence and genteel accomplishment. The less they appeared to know, the more attractive they were. Men looked for ignorance in their wives, not for intelligence, for a sentimental purity and submissiveness, not for character or excitement. A little drawing and painting, a little music and a lot of needlework which could be done quietly round the table in the evenings while papa read aloud from some improving book, gave the proper ladylike background for the hopeful girl waiting patiently for the right suitor to appear and be approved by the family, according to the law of filial obedience.

Music was the accomplishment most likely to win a husband. In the new suburban villas beginning to extend to Clapham, Streatham and Belsize Park, the upright piano with its fretted or inlaid front and twisted candelabra was the focus of the drawing-room. In the mornings the young ladies practised—those next door to Carlyle in Cheyne Row tortured him to such an extent when he was trying to work that he resorted to banging loudly on the party wall with a poker; but their practising was only the preliminary to their performance in the evening. A 'lovely touch' on the piano was admired, or the sweet, celestial sound of a harp brushed by even the most inexpert fingers which by association could be termed angelic. A slight tremolo in the voice added charm to the songs of Mendelssohn and sweetness to the popular English ballads that were published by the hundred every year: roses bloomed in magic gardens, lovers said a long farewell, romantic dreamers looked towards Eternity, and pale hands or pink blushes ravished the heart. What young man could resist such inducement? And, besides, in turning the pages or joining the duets and the trios, he could take part in the performance. It might well be his only chance of coming close to the girl he fancied would make him a wife.

Isambard Kingdom Brunel, the brilliant engineer of the Great Western Railway and the Clifton suspension bridge, was undoubtedly attracted to Mary Horsley by the music-making in her family home in Kensington, though this was of a much higher standard than in most households, since her father was an organist and one of her sisters such a talented pianist she could have become a professional if her family had not thought it immodest for her to appear in public. Mrs Horsley was kind and sensible; when Brunel called there, she invited him to stay to dinner, which he did with alacrity, finding this friendly household a delightful relaxation from his exacting work and his ambitious plans for the future. The two boys were charming and the three girls had rather more freedom than most, for besides their music and their parlour games, their mother permitted them to stroll round the garden with their friends on summer evenings until she flashed a lamp from her bedroom window as a warning that it was time for Mr Brunel to say goodnight. She also allowed them to go on an expedition to the Zoological Gardens in Regent's Park, the girls driving there in a fly while Brunel and his brother-in-law and a cousin called Thomas Hawes, rode on horseback. 'We did not see much of the animals,' Fanny wrote afterwards, 'for the gentlemen were all so very much fatigued that they sank down on some seats opposite the elephants and there remained until near dinner time. I was very glad,' she added, 'that they rested themselves in front of a decent animal, for some of them are very indelicate; indeed the monkeys are so very nasty that I told Thomas Hawes I would rather not look at them—really, with a gentleman, I think it quite indelicate.' Thomas Hawes thought so too, and he took Fanny to see the otters instead; swimming about in a rather grubby pond, they really behaved very nicely.

On all these expeditions and others in the leafy lanes round Holland Park, it might have been supposed that the family would have noticed how much attention young Mr Brunel was paying to Mary, the most beautiful though least talented of the sisters. The girls, however, only saw what they permitted themselves to see—it might have been indelicate to have noticed more; and both Fanny and Sophy were startled when they realized that their forceful and attractive visitor had made Mary an offer of marriage. They 'immediately fell into such fits of laughing' that Mary was quite hurt and obliged to leave them or she would have burst into tears. 'But really, *Love* is such a very new character in our family, not to speak of *marriage*, that I must have a little laugh,' Fanny wrote excitedly—and getting ready for the wedding brought fresh joy to the whole family. There were trips to Turner's the upholsterers and family furnishers, to make 'endless substantial purchases'; visits to the dressmaker and the milliner for gowns and shawls and new bonnets and a trousseau of underwear; and finally the exciting, overwhelming, nerve-racking day of the wedding itself.

Brunel had chosen wisely. He had found a wife who did not interfere with his passionate absorption in his work, yet one of whom he could be proud as he became more prosperous. Mary was an ornament to his success. He gave her a silk-lined carriage and a footman, expensive clothes and jewellery, which she wore with the elegance of a *grande dame*. He took pleasure in her appearance and in his three children without ever yielding one particle of the ambitious purpose, which had once persuaded him to declare 'my profession is after all my only fit wife'. If Mary was sometimes lonely when his work took him on long trips round the country or abroad, she had many compensations in the grandeur of her home. The dining-room of her house in Duke Street, Westminster, was adorned with frescoes of scenes from Shakespeare's plays painted by Landseer and her table with a massive silver-gilt centre-piece and side-pieces to match presented to her husband by a grateful Great Western Railway.

Mary had never known the bitterness of waiting for marriage to come her way—she had found it quickly and easily. To the girls in their late twenties who watched the years passing and the embarrassing manoeuvres of their parents to secure them husbands, the leisure they possessed was more of a nightmare than a pleasure. Beyond the age of thirty, nothing could be seen except a long, dark tunnel of diminishing returns: the frustration and the misery of the governess or the companion, the shame of the woman whose whole purpose in life had never been fulfilled, the sadness of the spinster and the maiden aunt and the drudgery of the dutiful daughter at home. Almost any husband was better than none—but not for that soaring eagle among the domestic hens of her generation—not for Florence Nightingale.

The daughter of well-to-do parents with high aristocratic connexions, she was expected to lead the life of a cultured young lady in town and country, to sit in the drawing-room with her mother and sister listening to their flow of trivial conversation, to do a little drawing and painting and some needlework and to make a good match with some young gentleman of her own class. Leisure lapped round her like the idle incoming tide of a calm sea—and she loathed it. 'Why write, read or paint when nothing can come of it?' she cried. 'Why be expected to look merry and to say something lively mornings, noons and nights?' And who could enjoy being read to, when it was like lying on one's back and having liquid poured down one's throat? 'Oh, weary days!' she wrote in the year of the Great Exhibition, when she was thirty. 'Oh, evenings that never seem to end— for how many years have I watched that drawing-room clock and thought it would never reach the ten! And for twenty, thirty years more to do this! Women don't consider themselves as human beings at all. There is absolutely no God, no country, no duty to them at all, except family. . . . I have known a good deal of convents and everyone has talked of the petty grinding tyrannies supposed to be exercised there, but I know of nothing like the petty grinding tyranny of a good English family. And the only alleviation is that the tyrannized submits with a heart full of affection.'

That was the trouble. Florence Nightingale did not really wish to displease her parents. She considered Richard Monckton Milnes, the last of the eligible suitors they put in her path, very seriously. 'I have an intellectual nature which requires satisfaction and that would find it in him,' she noted. 'I have a passional nature which requires satisfaction and that would find it in him. I have a moral, an active nature which requires satisfaction, and that would *not* find it in his life. . . . ' For a moment she wondered if the satisfaction of her 'passional nature' would be enough; then at once she realized that 'to be nailed to a continuation and exaggeration' of her present life would be worse than death. She must continue 'to dig after her little plan in silence', nursing the sick wherever she could and studying the detailed medical books her family thought were quite unfit for feminine eyes. Here was her only escape from the idle leisure of a well brought up young lady and the domestic routine of a married woman, the only fulfilment of her call from God to serve Him through serving humanity.

When the Crimean War broke out three years later, Florence Nightingale had managed to obtain some training as a nurse against the will of her family. No one and nothing could stop her. She arrived in Scutari in November 1854 and immediately began her work among the diseased and mutilated soldiers with a heroism and a genius for organization that left everyone gasping. If in the stench and the filth and the horror of her early days there she ever looked back to the spacious and sweet-smelling drawing-room at Embley where her mother and her sister still sat over their embroidery, it was without any regrets whatever. She had found her purpose in life and had dedicated herself to it. Monckton Milnes did not regret his failure to win her, either. 'If she had married me there would have been one heroine the less in the world and certainly not one hero the more,' he observed dryly, having wisely married the Hon. Annabel Crewe instead, a gentle, pretty young woman with an affectionate nature, who took pleasure in her home and was quite undisturbed by the compulsive driving force of Miss Nightingale.

8

MATRIMONY

IT WAS SURPRISING how much character and independence some early Victorian women did succeed in developing within the limits of the lives they were taught to accept by the unrelenting moral attitude of society. Far from crushing their individuality, the restrictions imposed upon them often allowed them to pursue their interests in their own time and at their own pleasure. Thus Elizabeth Barrett, isolated from the world by sickness and the insane, possessive affection of a tyrannical father, though she often described her room in Wimpole Street as a prison and herself as a walled-up nun or a bird in a cage, used every moment of her enforced leisure to concentrate on her poetry.

At the age of ten, she had already recognized that poetry was her vocation, 'an object to read, think and live for', and her young mind was full of 'nothing but the pleasures of literary success'. Twenty-five years later, in her mid-thirties, apparently suffering from some incurable nervous debility, she was still studying to improve her technique and to overcome her faults, which she candidly described to a *testa lunga*, or a headlong desire to rush precipitously forward 'through all manner of nettles and briars, instead of keeping to the path'—quite forgetting, or possibly not realizing, that in many ways her discipline was phenomenal. For how else could she have mastered seven languages, including Greek and Latin, almost alone, with only a few lessons here and there from her brother's tutor and by correspondence with an old, blind scholar? How else could she have devoured every book in her father's library through the long sleepless nights of her first illness and again through the terrible months at Torquay when she was too ill to leave her bed? Without the fierce discipline she exercised over her own mind and the intense pleasure she derived from reading and writing, she might well have given herself up to the mental and moral idleness of a confirmed invalid. Instead, when she returned to Wimpole Street in 1841, still half dead with grief at the loss of her favourite brother in a drowning accident off Babbacombe Bay and still so weak she could not lift her hand, she struggled to pursue her literary career with the intrepid courage of an explorer and the fanatical devotion of a saint.

For months on end she never left her room, lying on the sofa with her darling dog Flush at her feet and the windows so hermetically sealed against the air and the light they became quite overgrown with ivy. Her father came upstairs to visit her and to pray beside her in the morning and the evening, and was quite satisfied that no other kind of life would suit her frail constitution or his own obsessive devotion to her. Otherwise she saw no one, except her sisters and her remaining brothers, her personal maid Wilson and a few chosen friends, the kindly Miss Mitford and the good-natured Mr Kenyon being admitted privately to her room on very rare occasions. 'Books and thoughts and dreams and domestic tenderness can and ought to leave nobody lamenting,' she wrote, and when the wind blew the little leaves of the ivy against her window-pane, '*then* I think of forests and groves'. There was nothing else to look at or to look forward to in the long and lonely hours of the day; yet her isolation, combined with the opium prescribed by her doctors, stimulated her imagination to find release in the wild outbursts of creative activity that alone could satisfy her ardent spirit.

By 1844 she had two volumes of new poems ready for publication and a vast number of correspondents in the literary world to whom she wrote frequently with a vigorous intellectual delight. But it was not until five months after her *New Poems* had appeared, in January 1845, that she received her first letter from Robert Browning. 'I love your verses with all my heart, dear Miss Barrett,' he began without preamble, 'and this is no off-hand complimentary letter that I shall write—whatever else, no prompt matter-of-course recognition of your genius, and there a graceful natural end of the thing. . . .' And he went on with the same bold sincerity to repeat: 'I do, as I say, love these books with all my heart—and I love you too. Do you know I was once not very far from seeing you? Mr Kenyon said to me one morning, "Would you like to see Miss Barrett?" then he went to announce me—then he returned—you were too unwell, and now it is years ago, and I feel as if at some untoward passage in my travels, as if I had been close, so close, to some world's wonder in chapel or crypt, only a screen to push and I might have entered, but there was some slight, so it seems now, slight and just sufficient bar to admission, and the half-opened door shut, and I went home my thousands of miles, and the sight was never to be?'

Elizabeth's response was immediate. She wrote off by return of post: 'I thank you, dear Mr Browning, from the bottom of my heart. You meant to give me pleasure by your letter—and even if the object had not been answered, I ought still to thank you. But it is thoroughly answered. Such a letter from such a hand! Sympathy is dear—very dear to me: but the sympathy of a poet, and such a poet, is the quintessence of sympathy. . . . For the rest you draw me with your kindness. Is it indeed true that I was so near the pleasure and honour of making your acquaintance?—and can it be true that you look back on the lost opportunity with any regret? *But*—you know —if you had entered the "crypt", you might have caught cold, or been tired to death and *wished* yourself "a thousand miles off". . . . Winters shut me up as they do the doormouses's eyes; in the spring *we shall see.*'

More than that she could not at once allow in answer to Robert Browning's question mark. But a new and dazzling pleasure, utterly spontaneous and unlooked-for, had entered the pent-up life of the thirty-eight-year-old Miss Barrett with the beginning of their correspondence, which was soon to become more and more intimate as they discovered each other through the medium of their frank and self-revealing letters. She was naturally afraid of admitting so ardent an admirer to her presence, afraid of disappointing his high expectation; yet at last his gentle insistence that the spring had come could no longer be resisted, and on Monday, 20 May 1845, Browning called at Wimpole Street and was conducted privately to her room. He was not disappointed. If she saw herself as a faded invalid face to face with a virile, handsome man of thirty-three, he had no such thoughts of her, for this first visit to her darkened room enhanced the passionate tenderness he already felt for her and filled his heart with rapture.

All through the summer he called regularly, though in secret and as a 'friend', encouraging her to go out for little drives and walks with her sisters, enfolding her in a selfless, invigorating devotion that endowed her with new hope and gradually, as she came to realize the depth of his feeling for her, the promise of a new life altogether. Cruelly refused permission by her father to go abroad for her health, she had yet one more winter to endure in

Wimpole Street, but now she was no longer alone and no longer inhibited by doubts and fears. Browning's strength, his adoration and his optimism supported her, drawing her irresistibly on to that day in September 1846 when, half-fainting with excitement and fatigue and dosed on sal volatile by a nearby chemist, she met him at Marylebone Church and was secretly married to him. A week later she slipped out of the house with her little dog Flush and her trusted maid Wilson, and was on her way to Italy with her husband.

Time deepened their devotion to each other. From Pisa she wrote to a friend: 'We have been married two months and every hour has bound me to my husband more and more; if the beginning was well, still better is it now—that is what he says to me, and I say back again day by day'—and so it was all through their life together at the Casa Guidi in Florence, where Elizabeth gave birth to a son and their joy in each other endured until her death thirteen years later.

> O lyric love, half angel and half bird
> And all a wonder and a wild desire . . .

Thus in *The Ring and the Book* Browning immortalized his beloved and a romance that bore the stress and strain of reality without ever declining into the complacent monotony of a Victorian marriage.

Elizabeth Barrett Browning had found the courage to break out of a suffocating existence into a wider and more rewarding life. And she was not alone in this. Another woman writer of quite a different character sought fulfilment at the age of thirty-five in living with a man who was already married, thereby stepping outside the strict conventions of the age and wondering with surprise and indignation why some of her closest friends disapproved. Marian Evans, when she decided to live with George Henry Lewes, was already well known in the literary world for her conduct of the *Westminster Review*, her translations of the German philosophers and her forthright book reviews. Men admired her extraordinary intellectual brain, more masculine than feminine in its capacity for abstract thought; they liked her taste in music—she played the piano and sang extremely well; they shared her *avant garde* opinions in politics and theology and her high moral purpose in wishing to make the world a better place. Chapman, her publisher and the owner of the *Westminster Review*, in whose house she lodged in 1851, made love to her, though he was married and had his mistress living in the house as well as his wife and Marian; and Herbert Spencer found her a stimulating companion. 'I have known but few men with whom I could discuss a question in philosophy with more satisfaction,' he declared; and besides singing duets with her, he frequently took her to the opera or the concerts at Exeter Hall without a third party, or for long, inspiring walks by the river to Richmond and to Kew.

Yet in spite of her unique position as an unchaperoned woman in a world of men and in spite of her success at Chapman's literary soirées which increased the glamour of her reputation, Marian remained ill at ease, unhappy and frustrated. She still suffered from the headaches and the appalling fits of depression that had tormented her all her life. Once, as a girl in her twenties looking for comfort, she had underlined a bleak comment of Harriet Martineau's referring to 'the fortunate in sorrow', who had 'a new and delicious pleasure, which none but the disappointed can feel—the pleasure of rousing their souls to bear pain'. And this seemed to Marian to be her only hope of enduring her journey in life. She was deeply conscious of her lack of physical beauty, morbidly sensitive to her own real and imagined defects and at the same time 'possessed by the common yearning of

womanhood'. Having abandoned the ardent religious
faith of her girlhood, the desire of devoting herself to
some earthly cause had become an obsession, only surpassed by the desire to be of use and to belong to someone. Friendship was not enough, intellectual pleasure
gave no ultimate satisfaction; she believed she was
unwanted, unloved, doomed to a life of sorrow. And
when she first met Spencer's friend, George Henry
Lewes, his flippant manner did not attract her at all. She
thought he was ugly and said so in no uncertain manner.

Lewes was a clever journalist: 'an airy loose-tongued
merry-hearted being with more sail than ballast', according to Jane Carlyle, 'and the most amusing little fellow
in the whole world if you only look over his unparalleled
impudence which is not impudence at all but man-of-
genius *bonhomie*'. His reputation in London was un-
savoury. It was common knowledge that he had shared
his young wife with Thornton Hunt on Shelley's principle
of free love while looking elsewhere for his own pleasure,
which meant flinging himself into one frivolous affair
after another in a misguided attempt to disguise his own
unhappiness. With his long, fair moustache, his curled
hair and hollow cheeks, he was attractive to some
women and used 'the wonderful expressiveness of his
eyes' to some purpose. But by the time he confided his
secret misery to Marian Evans one afternoon in her room
at Chapman's house in the Strand, he was on the verge
of a nervous breakdown.

To Marian his declaration was a new dawn. She forgot
his ugliness, his reputation, his loose tongue and his
Frenchified manners in the one overwhelming glory of
his need. At once her affair with Chapman looked shoddy
and her pleasure in Spencer's company at the opera or the
play grew pale compared with Lewes's confidence in her;
and she lost no time in moving from the Strand to rooms
of her own near the Edgware Road. Here, all through the

autumn and the winter of 1853, Lewes could visit her in private and she could console him, mother him and remake his life for him. The difficulty was to explain what had happened. She now had to eat her words and to persuade her friends that Lewes was not what he seemed, but 'a man of heart and conscience wearing a mask of flippancy'. She expected them to believe her and was mortally offended when they did nothing of the kind. How could they be so obtuse? And how could they fail to understand that in her view, her moral integrity was in no way undermined by her decision to live with the man who needed her so desperately? Divorce from his wife was out of the question for Lewes and to lose him out of the question for Marian, so they did the only possible thing—they packed their bags and left for Germany in the summer of 1854.

In Weimar they met Liszt, 'a glorious creature in every way', and Marian wrote home 'I have had a month of exquisite enjoyment and seem to have begun life afresh', which was true. She had judged Lewes correctly. He was a delightful companion, a most loving and devoted husband, and she gave him the strength to reform his frivolous disposition through the more serious qualities of her heart and mind. It was only the rumours from London that disturbed her 'exquisite enjoyment'. Her former friends were saying that she had tempted Lewes to abandon his wife and children when, in fact, he was still helping to maintain them; they were saying she had lost her head over a worthless creature and was living in sin with a man everyone knew to be shallow, unstable and highly promiscuous in his relations with women. They could not, or would not recognize the truth as Marian saw it, or even address their letters to Mrs Lewes instead of to Miss Evans who, as she pointed out more than once, had now ceased to exist.

Back in England in 1855, she was still trying to justify

herself with a moral arrogance ill-suited to her equivocal position. 'If there is any action or relation in my life which is and always has been profoundly serious,' she wrote to her friend Caroline Bray, 'it is my relation to Mr Lewes. . . . Light and easily broken ties are what I neither desire theoretically nor could live for practically. Women who are satisfied with such ties do *not* act as I have done.' No amount of argument, however, could persuade even the advanced thinking Victorians to approve of her conduct, and it was not until five years later when she had written her first two successful books under the name of George Eliot, that she began to regain her former place in society. The metamorphosis in her reputation was quite extraordinary. By the time *Adam Bede* had gone into a third edition and the secret of her authorship had been divulged by a proud and triumphant Lewes, the high moral purpose revealed in her work could no longer be in doubt. The friends she had failed to convince by argument were put to shame. If they did not at once forgive her, they swallowed their disapproval and went out to Holly Lodge in Wandsworth to visit her, together with a number of new admirers and a whole bunch of young female disciples, who found her strong personality and her oracular judgement passionately exciting.

As her fame increased and she held court in her new home in St John's Wood, no high priestess could have enjoyed more reverence from her worshippers. Yet the original, morbid Marian Evans, the young woman who had found pleasure in rousing her soul to bear pain, persisted through all the furore she created as George Eliot. 'I feel no regret that fame, as such, brings no pleasure,' she wrote, 'but it *is* a grief to me that I do not constantly feel strong in thankfulness that my past life has vindicated its uses, and given me reasons for gladness that such an unpromising woman child was born into this world.' Even her association with Lewes, which lasted until his death in 1878 and gave her everything she desired or had hoped for, carried a hidden blight within it, since to any woman of her generation, even one who was recognized as a nation-wide moralist, there was no wholly satisfactory substitute for a lawful marriage.

No doubt this was partly the reason why Marian astonished the world a second time by marrying John Cross, who was young enough to be her son, within eighteen months of losing Lewes. She had known him some years and he had recently lost his mother; it was natural they should console each other while studying together to translate Dante's *Inferno*. But the consternation the marriage engendered among her friends was almost as great as the original shock she had given them in going away with Lewes. She had forced them reluctantly to regard him as the only love of her life, even to accept her irregular union with him—what could she expect them to think of this? Once again she had to explain. 'I wish that you already knew my husband better,' she wrote to Barbara Bodichon. 'His character is so solid, his feeling is so eminently delicate and generous. But you will have inferred something of this from his desire to dedicate his life to the remaining fragment of mine.' They went abroad to Venice, where they visited the opera and the theatre and the picture galleries, and Marian recovered sufficiently from her grief to take pleasure in her young husband's 'miraculous affection'; but back in London she caught cold at a concert in the new St James's Hall and three days later she was dead. Miss Edith Simcox, who often embarrassed Marian by lying on the floor to kiss her feet and wrote of her ecstatically as 'the love passion of my life', wept bitterly at her funeral and walked all the way home from Highgate Cemetery in the rain.

George Eliot had succeeded in living down the scandal caused by her behaviour through the unmistakable strength of her moral rectitude and the sheer weight of her didactic opinions. Effie Ruskin dared the ostracism of society by seeking a divorce from her husband as the innocent party in a marriage that was never consummated. Innocence, being the most highly esteemed quality in the feminine character, should have made Effie an object of sympathy; but divorce in any circumstances bore the terrible odium of misconduct, and as the Victorian age advanced towards new heights of ethical probity, any deviation from the recognized behaviour of married couples was viewed with horror, while inspiring the prurient with an inverted pleasure which they would not, perhaps, have been willing to admit. Victorian matrons surrounded by a brood of children in the safe domesticity of their own drawing-rooms and Victorian husbands enjoying their all-powerful situation as head of the family, could congratulate themselves that nothing so irregular had ever been permitted to cross the threshold of their lives. They did not approve of Effie Ruskin's boldness or of John Ruskin's lack of self-defence; still less of the young pre-Raphaelite painter, John Everett Millais. But disapproval did not stop them from following the unhappy details of the case with a certain relish.

Effie Gray had married John Ruskin when she was twenty, much to the dismay of John's possessive parents, whose maddening interference with their daughter-in-law filled her with a not unnatural resentment. Bewildered by her husband's inability or lack of desire to consummate the marriage, irritated by his intense concentration on his work, by his selfishness and his chronic extravagance in buying medieval illuminated manuscripts, which he locked away for fear of 'mortal fingers touching them' so that they were of no pleasure to Effie at all, she was desperately looking around for some way out of her misery when she first met Millais and acted as a model for his painting, 'The Order of Release'. He was the same age as herself; delicate, fascinating and, in the eyes of some people, a painter of genius. Ruskin admired his work sincerely; and at his suggestion Millais joined husband and wife on a holiday in the wilds of Scotland where, in the pouring rain, Millais fell in love with Effie and she confided her secret to him. He was appalled. 'I consider Ruskin's treatment of your daughter,' he wrote to Effie's mother, 'so sickening that for quietness' sake she should as much as possible prevent his travelling, or staying a summer in company with a friend, *who cannot but observe* his hopeless apathy in *everything regarding her happiness*. I cannot conceal the truth from you that she has more to put up with than any living woman.'

Other friends of Effie's felt the same. And in the summer of 1854, when she brought her case against Ruskin, it was they who enjoyed a vicarious excitement in the scandal it created. Lady Eastlake, the influential wife of the President of the Royal Academy, who was fond of Effie and hated Ruskin, took the utmost pleasure in acting as Effie's confidential adviser. She believed it was her duty to tell everyone the truth, rousing all her important friends in society to an hysterical pitch of indignation against Ruskin, which satisfied her own outraged feelings towards him. People took sides in the affair. 'Gentlemen retire into corners and talk it over,' Millais reported to Effie's mother, 'some expressing grief beyond utterance, placidly imbibing a cream ice, and one man in twenty, for the sake of peculiarity, voluntarily acts as counsel for the "Author of Modern Painters" and makes the best of his case.'

It was not often, however, that Millais was able to find the gossip amusing. He was far too sensitive and far too anxious to protect Effie, who prudishly kept him at a distance for much longer than was necessary after she had regained her freedom. When at last she consented to marry him, he lost his nerve altogether and she had to bathe his face in eau-de-Cologne on their honeymoon journey because 'he cried dreadfully, and instead of being happy and cheerful, seemed in despair'. He recovered his equilibrium in due course, and in time the marriage was accepted by society, though even after he had abandoned the pre-Raphaelite Brotherhood to become a respectable academician, Queen Victoria still refused to allow him to paint her portrait because she understood that 'he had seduced his future wife while painting her'. She would not consent to receive Effie at Court either, until 1896, when Princess Louise begged her to consider the dying painter's last request.

The repercussions on Ruskin's life were more serious than he at first realized. He was free to travel and to work and, aided by the claustrophobic affection of his parents, to foster the growth of his own egotism unencumbered by the demands of a discontented wife. 'I don't think myself a genius,' he wrote to his father in 1857, 'but there is a strong instinct in me to draw and describe the things I love. . . . I should like to draw St Mark's stone by stone, touch by touch'—and indeed his greatest pleasure lay in observing, describing and absorbing the works of art he loved so passionately. Year by year his reputation increased. As an art critic of great force and eloquence he came to be regarded as the high priest of Victorian taste, enjoying an authoritative position which was not challenged until Whistler took proceedings against him in 1878, after Ruskin had written of his art that he 'never expected to hear a coxcomb ask two hundred guineas for flinging a pot of paint in the public's face'. But his emotional life was a calamity, and when at the age of fifty he fell in love with the twenty-year-old Rose La Touche, he wrote: '*If a second* time an evil report goes forth about my marriage—my power of doing good by any teaching may be lost—and lost for ever . . . the question is a fearful one whether I might not thus confirm the calumnies before arising out of my former history.'

The question was never resolved—Rose La Touche refused him and broke his heart. But by this time the sexual relationship between man and woman had become so entangled in a web of prudery, hypocrisy and narrow-minded thinking, that Ruskin was by no means wrong about his power of doing good being lost for ever if he again exposed himself to the gossip of Victorian society. Dickens found himself in a similar dilemma when he fell in love with Ellen Ternan, his 'sweet, angelic' little actress. He, also, was approaching the dangerous age of fifty when he engaged her and her mother and sister to play in one of his elaborate amateur theatrical productions in Manchester; and at least one of his contemporaries— Thackeray—left it on record that his infatuation with the nineteen-year-old Ellen, rather than his dependence on his sister-in-law Georgina Hogarth, was the cause of the break-up of his marriage in 1858.

Whatever the reason, Kate who had once been his 'dearest mouse', became his 'skeleton in the cupboard', and the incompatibility of temperament between them was suddenly blown up into crisis when the bracelet Dickens intended to give Ellen was delivered by mistake to his wife. Kate lost her temper and stormed and cried, while her sister Georgina, who had been quietly making herself indispensable to Charles, took his side in the affair. She, not Kate, was the mistress of his house and she was clever enough to make a friend of Ellen, but Dickens himself behaved like a madman. Instead of keeping quiet, he wrote a bombastic letter of self-justification which got into the American newspapers. Referring to Ellen and the suspicion his final separation from his wife had cast upon him, he said: 'Two wicked persons [his mother-in-law and her third daughter] who should have spoken differently of me in consideration of earned respect and gratitude have (as I am told and indeed to my personal knowledge) coupled with the separation the name of a young lady for whom I have great attachment and regard. Upon my soul and honour there is not on this earth a more virtuous and spotless young lady. I know her to be innocent and pure and as good as my own dear daughters. I will not repeat her name—I honour it too much. Further I am quite sure that Mrs Dickens having received this assurance from me must now believe it, in the respect that I know her to have for me, and in the perfect confidence I know her in her better moments to repose in my truthfulness.'

Dickens was not a great imaginative writer for nothing —he believed every word he wrote, and he hated hypocrisy. Yet he had manoeuvred himself into a position where he could only pursue his pleasure to its ultimate end by deceiving the world that now venerated his books and viewed him as a doughty champion of the good against the evil in mankind. He was a world-wide figure, a husband of twenty years' standing and the father of ten children. Ellen Ternan's sweet blue eyes, her youth and her adoration made him feel a young man again, but he knew the world too well to risk an explosion with his devoted public. Whether or not under an assumed name, he actually kept Ellen as his mistress in a little house in Peckham, has never been proved. The lack of letters between them would seem to suggest that Dickens was careful enough to destroy any evidence that could have been brought against him, and the strain of leading a double life could well have been partly the cause of his almost insane passion for showing himself off in public during the last years of his life. Ellen perhaps was innocent—perhaps not. She married a curate six years after Dickens's death and helped her husband to run a school in Margate, earning the respect and the affection of everyone who knew her and never yielding her secret.

The Moloch of middle-class morality was appeased. Kate Dickens, the sacrificial victim, deserted by her husband and her children, lived on alone, without the status of a wife or a widow.

The status of a Victorian wife was often the salve to her suppressed feelings, and keeping up appearances of greater importance than the expression of her own likes and dislikes. It was her duty to submit to her husband and to bear one child after another—often as many as twelve or thirteen—without complaint and irrespective of the effect on her health. But for many wives the duty was also a pleasure. Motherhood was the sacred function of the female species. Lying on the sofa, expecting or recovering from the event, the wives had plenty of leisure to reflect with satisfaction on what they had achieved, and if their husbands sometimes sought pleasure on the side, they could take shelter under the convenient umbrella of belief that God made man a more promiscuous creature than woman. It was only when the woman saw her man making a fool of himself that she found it difficult to control her displeasure and not to show by her manner what she was feeling.

Jane Carlyle, with no children to absorb her time, only her maids and her little dog Nero, suffered intensely when her famous husband came under the spell of Lady Ashburton—and this was apparently a platonic pleasure, the devotion of an egotist to a formidable, middle-aged lady of great wealth and power, whose social standing was high above the simplicity of his own home. 'That eternal Bath House', Jane wrote in her journal in 1855. 'I wonder how many thousand miles Mr C. has walked between there and here, putting it altogether; setting up always another milestone betwixt himself and me. Oh, good gracious! when I first noticed that heavy yellow house without knowing, or caring to know, who it belonged to, how far I was from dreaming that through years and years I should carry every stone's weight of it on my heart.'

It was not funny either, when 'old Rogers, who ought to have been buried long ago, so old and ill-natured is he grown', sat down beside her at a dinner-party and said: 'I want to ask you, my dear, is your husband as much infatuated as ever with Lady Ashburton? And do *you* like her—tell me honestly, is she kind to *you*—as kind as she is to your husband?' Jane did her best to laugh the whole thing off. 'A very devilish old man! but he got no satisfaction to his devilishness out of *me*,' she commented—though, in fact, she was seldom treated with anything more than condescension by Lady Ashburton, who cultivated the society of eminent men at the expense of their wives. Once when Carlyle bullied her into going to a ball at Bath House, she was thrown into 'a perfect fever' about buying a new white silk dress and having it cut down to 'the due pitch of indecency', but as soon as she got into the fine rooms 'amongst the universally *bare* people', she felt so much 'in keeping' with them she forgot her embarrassment.

'I was glad *after* that I went,' she wrote to Helen Welsh, 'not for any pleasure I had at the time, being past dancing and knowing few people—but it is an additional idea of life to have seen such a party—all the Duchesses one ever heard tell of blazing in diamonds, all the young beauties of the season, all the distinguished statesmen etc. . . . What pleased me best was the good look I got *into the eyes* of the old Duke of Wellington—one has no notion, seeing him in the streets what a dear kind face he has.' But there was yet one word more Jane added to her letter, describing her hostess in one of her most caustic understatements. 'Lady Ashburton receiving all these people with her grand-Lady airs, was also a sight worth seeing,' she concluded. She could not—and never did— quite forgive Mr C. his attraction to Bath House, for this went far beyond her general acceptance of his view that in marriage it was 'in the nature of the woman to cling to the man for support and direction, to comply with his humours and feel pleasure in doing so, simply because they are his.' After all it depended on where his humours were likely to lead him.

But Lady Ashburton, whatever Jane may have thought about her, was a very successful hostess and for the man of letters or the social climber, an invitation to Bath House was a high honour. For the politically ambitious, Cambridge House not far away in Piccadilly, was another, even more desirable mecca. Here, the former Emily Cowper, who at the age of fifty-two had married Lord Palmerston, stood at the top of the stairs with her husband to receive the guests. 'Always very smart and looking so well in her diamonds, with her head held high' and a watchful eye on the company, this great lady entertained everyone of note in the diplomatic and political world, always with a view to helping her fiery-tempered lord in the ups and downs of his career as England's greatest statesman. With her subtle feminine intuition, she knew exactly how to undermine his enemies, how to soothe his friends and provide the right kind of atmosphere at her parties for his pleasure and her own.

This late marriage between the promiscuous Regency beau, called 'Cupid' when he had waltzed with Mme de Lieven at Almack's, and the still beautiful widow of Panshanger, was, in fact, a love match, crowning a romance of thirty years' standing and continuing for another quarter of a century into old age. On their honeymoon Emily wrote that Palmerston was 'so completely happy that it was quite a pleasure to look at him'; and twenty-four years later, after a long sitting in the House lasting well beyond midnight, an observer saw the eighty-year-old Prime Minister vanish upstairs towards the Ladies' Gallery to embrace his 'dearest love' with the ardour of a young man.

Palmerston crossed the Queen many times in spite of Emily's wise advice begging him 'not to enter into argument with her, but to lead her on gently by letting her believe you have both the same opinions and the same wishes, but sometimes take different ways to carry them out'; yet he ruled Victorian England for ten years with great vigour and self-confidence, enjoying his power to the utmost and sharing it with his wife. A malicious writer suggested that when Emily forgot her rouge and Palmerston omitted to dye his whiskers, a real crisis in the affairs of England could be inferred. But the truth was that their pleasure in each other gave them both the spirit of eternal youth and made them immune from outside criticism. The world changed round them: they survived it hand in hand, alone on the great staircase, when the guests had gone and the lights at Cambridge House were extinguished after the party was over.

9

ADVENTURES

in

ECCENTRICITY

PALMERSTON WAS STILL Prime Minister of England
when a calamity befell the Queen from which she was
never wholly to recover. In 1861, worn out by his
incessant toil for the benefit of the nation and distressed
by his eldest son's peccadilloes at Cambridge, the Prince
Consort fell ill and died quite suddenly. The Queen was
forty-two: her despair was alarming. What was worse,
she blamed the Prince of Wales for his father's death
instead of her own obstinacy in relying on the wrong
diagnosis of her elderly physician, Sir James Clark.
According to Lord Clarendon, she had 'an inconquer-
able aversion to her eldest son which was a positive
monomania with her . . . and I believe the poor boy
knows of his mother's dislike of him,' he added, 'but
seems to have the good taste not to speak of it.'

The young Prince was certainly in no doubt of the
fact that he had seldom, if ever, succeeded in pleasing his

father, which meant that he had seldom succeeded in pleasing his mother either. From his earliest childhood he had shown unmistakable signs of his Hanoverian ancestry in his desire for affection and sympathy, in his passionate temper and his preference for enjoying himself to concentrating on his studies. Consequently every outburst of high spirits in the boy had been firmly chastised, and every inclination towards expressing his true nature suppressed by both parents in their misguided endeavour to mould him into the image of his father. Now, in the Queen's saddest hour, he did his best to comfort her. But the Queen could not be comforted. 'There is no one to call me Victoria now,' she lamented. 'I only lived through him, my heavenly Angel. . . . Now I feel as though I am dead.'

Extravagant in her grief as in her joy, the Queen went into deep mourning and wore her widow's weeds for the next forty years to the very end of her long life. She forced herself to do her duty with courage and determination, but of pleasure there was none, except in the sentimental deification of her lost German Prince, in her memories of him at Windsor or Balmoral, where nothing was changed in his bedroom and by her command his evening clothes were laid out upon the bed every night as if he still had need of them. The Prince of Wales was sent off on a tour of the Holy Land and Egypt, where it was hoped that his elderly entourage would see that he behaved with a proper decorum. Two years later he was married to the Princess Alexandra of Denmark and given his own establishment at Marlborough House.

The effect of the Queen's withdrawal from public life was to focus society on Marlborough House instead. The Prince of Wales and his bride were young, good-looking and gay, and the Prince, whose gregarious instincts had been thwarted by his parents, took great pleasure in exercising the social sovereignty that was now his prerogative. Marlborough House glittered with wealth and luxury; etiquette was strict without being oppressive; grace, dignity and charm made up for lack of intellectual brilliance in this new royal household. The Prince studied the enjoyment of his friends and went racing with them at Ascot, Epsom and Goodwood, or on visits to their country houses for the hunting and shooting. He was a good sportsman, a gay companion and a *bon vivant* and, like his great uncle the Prince Regent, could seldom resist the attraction of a pretty woman. He did, however, conduct his affairs with more discretion, at least in the early years of his marriage, bearing in mind the moral temper of his own time in contrast to that of his forbears.

Not that the gas-lit London of the sixties was without its frivolous side. The unashamed sensuality of Harriette Wilson and her sisters had long since slipped under cover, but there were still the 'flash cribs' in the Haymarket frequented by the more bedraggled street-walkers and still the 'pretty horse-breakers' in Hyde Park, girls who worked in with a livery stable and were loosed on Rotten Row for the appraisal of the onlookers. To some they presented a spectacle of vice that was shocking to a degree, since the success they enjoyed disproved the Evangelical theory that prosperity and sin could not go together. To others, like George Augustus Sala, they were a perpetual source of delight. 'Can any scene in the world equal Rotten Row at four in the afternoon and in the full tide of the season?' he wrote. 'Watch the sylphides as they fly or float past in their ravishing riding-habits and intoxicatingly delightful hats; some with the orthodox cylindrical beaver with the flowing veil, others with roguish little wide-awakes, or pretty cocked cavaliers' hats and green plumes. And as the joyous cavalcade streams past . . . from time to time the naughty wind will flutter the skirt of a habit and display a tiny coquettish brilliant little boot with a military heel, and tightly strapped over it, the Amazonian riding trouser.'

As soon as these ladies of pleasure had captured a gentleman willing to protect them, they were tucked away in the new little villas in St John's Wood, where the high-walled gardens gave privacy to their visitors. The lilac and the laburnum bloomed in the spring and the once holy wood of the knights of St John tinkled with their laughter, their gaiety and their fun, while Victorian London frowned and continued its sober search for some moral nostrum that would bring these unrepentant 'fallen women' to salvation. Miss Howard, one of the prettiest horse-breakers ever to ride, lived discreetly in St John's Wood with her immensely rich lover Major Mountjoy Martin, before going to Paris with Prince Louis Napoleon, who kept her in a small house linked to his official residence at the Elysée by a garden door. And but for the arrival in Paris of Mlle Eugenie de Montijo, she might have married her Prince when he became Emperor. Instead she was forced into retirement at the Château de Beauregard and spent the remaining years of her life trying to get him to repay the six million gold francs she had gladly put at his disposal when she still believed she might become his Empress.

Catherine Walters, otherwise known as Skittles, was luckier. Brilliant and beautiful, with large violet-coloured eyes of a melting sweetness, a slender waist and sensitive hands, she had started life in a skittle-alley in Liverpool and came to London in the sixties, where she immediately fascinated the Marquis of Hartington, heir to the 7th Duke of Devonshire. Not only a fearless equestrienne, she drove her Orloff black ponies round the Park in superb style; and although she could swear like a fishwife and often did, men were bowled over by her tantalizing personality. The Marquis of Hartington gave her a splendid house in Mayfair and an annuity of £2,000 a year, which she enjoyed until her death shortly after the

First World War, but she was never at a loss for other admirers. At one moment in her career she ran away to New York with Aubrey de Vere Beauclerk, at another she enslaved the Prince of Wales and was adored by the poet Wilfrid Scawen Blunt, who wrote his *Love Sonnets of Proteus* in praise of her as 'a woman most complete in all the ways of loving', and prodigal of love—

> Brave as a falcon and as merciless . . .
> Untamed, unmated, high above the press.

Long after their rapturous love affair had ended, Blunt continued to visit her as a devoted friend; and when she was old, Lord Kitchener of Khartoum was to be seen among the circle of her adorers, proudly pushing her round the Park in a bath-chair. But perhaps Skittles's greatest triumph was her conquest of Mr Gladstone, who took tea with her and asked her advice on the work he was doing to reform the London prostitutes.

Gladstone's nocturnal rambles in the streets were open to misinterpretation. It was not pleasure he sought when he stopped and spoke to the gaudy women standing around the doorways of Mayfair, or only the pleasure of doing good; for it was his habit to persuade them to go home with him to Carlton House Terrace, where his charitable wife Catherine endeavoured to point out to them the error of their ways. Catherine never failed her husband in this awkward situation or any other, though it cannot have been easy to welcome such guests in a house full of respectable servants and with her own children asleep upstairs. Had she been the kind of Victorian matron to whom charity was a matter of sitting on committees in upper-class drawing-rooms, she would have been daunted by the prospect—but she was not; she combined indomitable courage with imagination and an eccentric individuality in all her good works, and had a genuine sympathy for the girls her husband brought home. It was not for nothing that in her family she was affectionately nicknamed Aunt Pussy.

Most Victorian women preferred to shut their eyes altogether to the whole idea of sex as a pleasure and their husbands, once they had begotten a sufficient number of children, found it convenient to encourage their blindness. If the divans and the bagnios of London failed to stimulate, perhaps a little jaunt to Paris could be arranged on some business or another which required personal attention. The boulevards glittered more brightly than the London streets and the scent of patchouli was wafted from the doll-like *demi-mondaines* with their frizzed-up hair, their frills and furbelows, and their tight little high-heeled boots tapping an unmistakable invitation as they trotted along the *pavé*. Wilkie Collins, alone or with Dickens for a companion, was by no means the only Englishman to find the Paris of the Emperor Louis Napoleon a pleasant change from the England of Queen Victoria. His adventures in search of entertainment often led him into compromising situations, but what did it matter in France where everyone spoke a foreign language and a man's character was enhanced by his degree of amorous prowess?

The 4th Marquis of Hertford, after a dissolute career in Regency England, had long been a resident in Paris, with two official mistresses: Mrs George Idle, the pretty widow of his closest friend, and Mlle Bréart, a ravishing girl of a cultured French family, to whom he was 'married' in 1834 by his own valet disguised as a clergyman. Louise Bréart always wore white, perhaps to remind her lover of this sacrilegious ceremony, and continued to do so when she was approaching the age of eighty; but she was faithful to her Marquis and a brilliant hostess at his exquisite house filled with the rare and beautiful works of art it was his pleasure to collect at Bagatelle on the Seine.

Richard Wallace, Lord Hertford's natural son from an earlier *engouement* with an English girl, was also a resident at Bagatelle, without being aware of his origin until his father died and left him his entire fortune. His own youthful affair with a shop-girl, Mlle Julie Castelnau, who bore him a child, was far more disastrous than any of his father's entanglements, for he was a man of the highest probity and, after Lord Hertford's death, he made a respectable woman of his mistress and brought her back to England as his wife. Victorian society accepted this coarse, cantankerous woman, who refused to speak anything but French, as the châtelaine of Hertford House and of Sudborn Hall in Suffolk. But she tormented the husband to whom she had once sold perfume long ago in Paris, turned against her son in favour of her secretary, John Murray Scott, and, immensely rich after her husband's death, was persuaded by Scott to leave the treasures of the Wallace Collection to the nation. Sir Richard seldom complained of his wife's capriciousness, even when she feigned illness rather than entertain the Prince of Wales at Sudborn, yet he must have wondered very often why he had ever been tempted as a young man to look for pleasure in the sulky, ill-tempered old woman Julie Castelnau had become.

Many temptations denied to them at home or carefully concealed in the background of their otherwise regular lives attracted the English to Paris. Monckton Milnes, the ex-suitor of Florence Nightingale, went there in search of erotic literature to add to his library at Fryston Hall in Yorkshire. As a young man at Cambridge in a circle of intellectual friends which included Alfred Tennyson and the short-lived Arthur Hallam, he had shown promise as a poet; but encouraged by his social aspirations and his love of leisure, he had grown into an amiable dilettante, a connoisseur of the arts and a not very successful politician, described by his American friend

Henry Adams as 'one of the two or three men in London who went everywhere, knew everybody and talked of everything'. By 1863, when he was given a peerage and took the title of Lord Houghton, his breakfast parties at Upper Brook Street and his house parties at Fryston had become the most distinguished feature of an otherwise rather dull decade of social entertainment. Certainly he had a genius for friendship and for mixing his talented friends together. On one occasion Thackeray's daughter when very young found the Archbishop of York at Fryston in the same party as Algernon Swinburne, who looked 'like Apollo or a fairy prince' and whose reading of his verses so shocked the Archbishop it was only when the butler, 'like an avenging angel', suddenly threw open the door and announced 'Prayers! my Lord!' that the situation was saved.

To the Archbishop, Lord Houghton's scholarly library at Fryston may have looked harmless enough. To Swinburne, Richard Burton and a few other of his chosen intimates, his hidden collection of *erotica* was fascinating and unique. It contained innumerable eighteenth-century French and Italian books and pictures, and all the known works of the 'odiously famous' Marquis de Sade. 'He is *the* Sadique collector of European fame', Swinburne wrote excitedly, and indeed it was often with some risk to his reputation that Lord Houghton managed to satisfy his curious delinquent pleasure in the aberrations of sex and cruelty. Apart from his regular trips to Paris, he employed as his agent a dubious English gentleman by the name of Frederick Hankey, who lived in the Rue Lafitte with a blowsy French mistress and was an expert at hunting up the rare volumes Lord Houghton coveted. The difficulty of getting these books through the English customs without their being seized was solved in various ways—by gumming the pages lightly together or inserting them in false bindings, and by Mr Harris, the manager of Covent Garden Theatre and a frequent traveller backwards and forwards to Paris, who was a past master at concealing a quarto volume 'in the bend of his back'.

Lord Houghton wondered afterwards whether he had been wise to introduce Swinburne to the works of de Sade or to his friend Richard Burton, for Burton encouraged Swinburne to drink and de Sade became an obsession with him. The young poet with his flaming red hair, white face and glittering green eyes, was already a grave problem to his parents. Admiral Swinburne had reluctantly given him permission to take up writing as a career after his failure at Oxford, Lady Jane worried about his health and his wild habits. At home they doctored him with tonics and champagne, but he could find 'no one to speak to and nothing to do beyond the family wall'. At Fryston he was more in his element and to Houghton's friend, Henry Adams, resembled 'a tropical bird, high-crested, long-beaked, quick moving, with rapid utterance and screams of humour, quite unlike any English lark or nightingale'. The shy American visitor had, in fact, never seen anyone like Swinburne before and the parties at Fryston astonished him. 'In 1862,' he remarked, 'even when ladies were not in the house, smoking was forbidden and guests usually smoked in the stables or the kitchen; but Monckton Milnes was a licensed libertine who let his guests smoke in the bedroom . . . and there, after dinner, all sat—or lay—till far into the night, listening to the rush of Swinburne's talk.' He recited Sophocles and Shakespeare 'forward and backward, from end to beginning', Dante, Villon, Victor Hugo and his own unpublished ballads, and everyone found him 'quite original, wildly eccentric, astonishingly gifted and convulsively droll'. Everyone except Admiral Swinburne and Lady Jane, who were naturally bewildered by their strange, frenetic offspring.

Lord Houghton gave him the encouragement he needed at that moment in his career and Swinburne responded with an almost frightening ardour; but the power and the passion in his poetry and its sadistic inspiration soon went far beyond Lord Houghton's comprehension and the friendship between them that blazed with such intensity in the sixties was extinguished by the time Swinburne published his *Songs before Sunrise*. The poet's gratitude turned to peevishness and a strong aversion to criticism. His old friend's good advice made him irritable, and until he met Theodore Watts Dunton, who set about taming his wild spirit with an irresistible reforming zeal, he preferred the society of his more Bohemian companions. With Captain Richard Burton especially, he could indulge in every excess his vivid and restless imagination painted as desirable, though very often pleasure proved as elusive as a mirage in the desert.

Burton himself was one of the most strange and savage eccentrics of the mid-Victorian Age. He was driven by a saturnine, neurotic temperament to satisfy his restless curiosity in the shadier corners of the Orient, yet was an explorer of genius and a man capable of inspiring a passionate devotion in his English wife. Isabel had first encountered him in 1851 at Boulogne, where her well-bred, impecunious Roman Catholic family, the Arundells, were trying to live economically before launching their daughters on the tide of London society. With her mind already set alight by the prophetic utterance of a gypsy who had promised her 'a wild and lawless life beyond the seas', she at once recognized her destiny in the strange figure walking towards her along the ramparts of the fusty little seaport. 'He was dressed in a black, short, shaggy coat, and shouldered a short thick stick, as if he were on guard'—and Isabel had time to notice a great deal more about him. 'He had very dark hair; black, clearly defined eyebrows; a brown weather-beaten complexion; straight *Arab* features; a determined mouth and chin nearly covered by an enormous moustache . . . and a fierce, proud, melancholy expression.' Yet all this was as nothing beside the burning fever of his large, black, flashing eyes. 'He looked at me as if he could read me through and through in a moment,' Isabel noted in her journal; and not content with looking, he took a piece of chalk out of his pocket and scrawled a message on the wall asking: 'May I speak to you?' 'No,' she replied with the same piece of chalk, 'Mother will be angry'—and Mother was angry; but fortunately some cousins gave a tea party and a dance and Richard was there 'like a star among the rushlights'. He spoke to her and danced with her—Isabel kept the sash she had worn where his arm had rested round her waist and her gloves that his hands had clasped and never put them on again; then he vanished on his daring pilgrimage to Mecca.

Isabel dropped back into the dull life of a young lady of leisure and greatly distressed her mother by persistently refusing to show the slightest interest in any of her suitors. She took no pleasure in being admired, though everyone thought her extremely handsome, and none in the balls and fêtes of the London season. She hated needlework, beadwork, embroidery and all the other pursuits that were considered a suitable occupation for a girl of her class, but did manage to steal and smoke some of her father's cigars in imitation of what she imagined Richard might be doing somewhere far away. Everything else bored her; she grew pale and listless and was seen by the doctor, who prescribed anti-dyspeptic pills which, of course, were of no use whatever for the complaint she was suffering from. Nothing excited her, except the rumours of Burton's exploits as they filtered back from the East, and while these were intoxicating, they also added to her frustration and her yearning to share 'a dry crust, privations, pain, danger with him I love'.

What the man she had set her heart on was actually doing in the Orient she could only guess. It was four years before she saw him again and found those 'terrible magnetic eyes' and his 'air of repressed ferocity' more fascinating than ever. He had achieved his incredible pilgrimage to the Holy Shrine of Mahomet and from Mecca had travelled back to Egypt, dallying in Cairo to begin a translation—and to sample—the *Thousand Nights and a Night* of Arabian debauchery and erotic adventure. Then he had gone off to India and from there on a dangerous expedition to Harar in Abyssinian Somaliland. Poor Isabel! She hung over the books he had written until she knew every word of them, and when at last he came home and they met again in the Botanical Gardens, accidentally or by fate, she surprised him by her intimate knowledge of his wanderings. He proposed to her and she accepted. But he was off again at the end of a fortnight to darkest Africa to explore the Great Lakes in search of the true source of the Nile, returning at last haggard and exhausted by fever, 'a skeleton figure, his yellow skin hanging in bags, his eyes protruding and his lips drawn away from his teeth'—yet still, as Isabel wrote in her diary, 'my earthly God and King! I could have knelt at his feet and worshipped him', she went on, and while watching over him and nursing him back to health: 'I used to like to sit and look at him and think, "*You are mine*, and there is no man on earth the least like you.'

There wasn't. Once more she had to let him go—this time to cross the American continent to visit the Mormons, while she on the pretext of needing a change of air, went into the country and set about training herself for life with Richard by learning to ride astride, to milk cows and groom horses, to shoot and wield a sword. At length her earthly God returned and one morning in 1861 she slipped away from home in a white bonnet and a fawn silk crinoline to the Bavarian Catholic Church in

Warwick Street, where Burton, looking like an Asiatic tiger dressed in a Victorian frock coat, was waiting for her on the steps. They went to visit Monckton Milnes at Fryston, sure of his sympathy if of no one else's, for it was a long time before the Arundells could bring themselves to accept their daughter's marriage and Burton did not easily fit in with life in England. 'I have undertaken a very peculiar man,' Isabel wrote with pride and not without some truth; and with her family connexions in high society, she immediately set about trying to obtain a good post for her husband abroad. The Foreign Office, however, chose to send the most brilliant Orientalist and explorer of his time to a dead end consular post in West Africa and then to Brazil, and it was not until 1869 that Burton was appointed to Damascus.

Isabel's cup of pleasure was full. 'I am to live among Bedouin Arab chiefs!' she exclaimed. 'I shall smell the desert air; I shall have tents, horses, weapons'—and of course, Richard. Richard in Arab robes, his fierce eyes gleaming from under his burnous, and herself disguised, she fondly believed, as Richard's son, though her somewhat matronly mid-Victorian figure thrust into a Syrian get-up with baggy trousers cannot have deceived many of the tribesmen she visited with her beloved husband. Rather than let him out of her sight, she endured sleeping in her clothes with a loaded revolver beside her or holding his horse when he entered a mosque to pray, and in the still evenings under the stars, she was enraptured when he allowed her to lie on a cushion at his feet and minister to his needs. No other Englishwoman, except Lady Hester Stanhope and Jane Digby El Mezrab, had ever entered into the life of the Orient with more enthusiasm; few other women had ever grasped their pleasure with such greedy insatiable fingers.

Lady Hester belonged to the eighteenth century; Jane Digby still lived in Damascus with her husband, Sheikh

Abdul Medjuel El Mezrab, and though she sometimes found Isabel naïve, it was possible in the East, as it would not have been in Kensington, for the two ladies to become friends and for Isabel to overlook Jane Digby's outrageous past. Born into Regency England and married young to the cynical Lord Ellenborough who was twice her age, this astonishing and beautiful creature with ravishing blue eyes and long fair hair had followed her instinct for pleasure by galloping madly eastwards across Europe, collecting two more husbands, three Kings and a number of other illustrious lovers on the way, until finally, at the age of forty-six, her adventurous journey had ended in marriage to her fourth and last husband, Sheik Abdul Medjuel El Mezrab. Lord of his tribe, Medjuel was a man of honour, brains and breeding. He proposed to Jane as he was escorting her across the desert to Palmyra—Jane was wearing a crimson velvet pelisse and a green satin riding-habit; and for twenty-five years she was supremely happy sharing a black Bedouin tent with him and the splendid house she had built in Damascus.

Isabel Burton could '*not* understand the contact with that black skin'—it made her shudder to think of an Englishwoman *married* to even the most charming and elegant of Arab chiefs. But she envied Jane Digby's complete identification with the East and had reason to be grateful for her friendship in 1871, when Richard got into trouble with some English missionaries on a visit to Syria and these same 'Bible Bangers' as he furiously dubbed them, reported him to his enemies at home. There was already an ample dossier filed away in the Foreign Office of the indiscretions Burton had committed at his post; now bishops and bankers in league together as representatives of the Victorian worship of God and Mammon exerted their influence, and without a word of warning or explanation, Her Majesty's Consul was dismissed and superseded overnight. He left Damascus at once, ordering his wife 'to pay, pack and follow', which she did, her anguish at leaving the Orient only very slightly relieved by her furious determination to fight for her husband's reinstatement.

This she did with a tireless obstinacy that wore down her enemies until they gave way under the overwhelming weight of her holy crusade to re-establish Richard's reputation. She took him around to house parties in the country and dinner parties in town that he might be seen by the right people in the right setting, which, alas, was always the wrong setting for this farouche follower of Mahomet. For Burton's life was over when he turned his back on the East in 1871 and he was a prisoner; Isabel had locked him in with her devotion, and her zeal to show him off as a great man without a flaw in his character smothered the activity of his remaining years. He accepted the consular post in Trieste that she had wrung out of the Foreign Office for him, was knighted by Queen Victoria and made a great deal of money out of his translation of the *Thousand Nights and a Night*, privately printed with copious notes drawn from his own experience, which Isabel piously promised not to read since they revealed what no virtuous woman should know. This indeed was all that was left to him—memories of the scandalous debauchery of the East, of the splendour, the cruelty, the erotic adventures and the strange mystic glory . . . memories of the secret, shameless pleasures of the past.

He spent hour upon hour brooding over his papers and his journals or stooping over his manuscripts, translating and annotating *The Scented Garden* of the Sheik el Nafzawih, his *magnum opus*, written with his 'life's blood'—and he died the day he finished it. But he had not reckoned with Isabel; he had not reckoned with her increasing religious mania nor with her determination that his name should live untarnished for ever. She shut herself up in his study for fourteen days and locked the door—and at the end of that time, she took the manuscript of *The Scented Garden* and burnt it, together with all his journals and his private papers.

'I never spoke to her or wrote to her after that irreparable act,' the novelist Ouida commented, for she believed that the enigmatic force and the wonderful originality of Burton's genius would have been disclosed in his private journals. And she added a further remark which would have shocked his widow profoundly if she had known of it. 'His masterful powers were tied up like great dogs in their kennels,' she said, 'and became savage as dogs become.' Or did Isabel know? Did she realize that in possessing him to gratify her own pleasure, she had destroyed her earthly God and King? Did she know that in spite of the gypsy's prediction of her lawless life beyond the seas, Mrs Grundy had caught up with her in the end?

10

FICTION

and

FASHION

IT WAS IN the romantic fiction of the time that many
of the stay-at-home Victorian women found diversion
and a vicarious satisfaction of their desires. When Mr
Mudie established his Select Lending Library in 1842, he
was doing them a great service, for those who could not
afford to buy the expensive three-decker volumes of
romance at a guinea and a half could borrow them instead
and were thus able to enjoy 'the nice large handsome
books that none but the *élite* could obtain', and with
them a sense of equality with the upper-class lady of
leisure. Moreover Mr Mudie guaranteed that nothing
offensive or in questionable taste would ever appear on
his shelves. 'Would you or would you not give that book
to your sister of sixteen to read?' he asked himself, and
the answer in the case of *The Ordeal of Richard Feverel* by
George Meredith and *The Morals of Mayfair* by Mrs Annie
Edwardes was no. Sensation without sex, romantic

sentiment and, in the final pages, the downfall of the
wicked and the eternal blessedness of the good were the
ingredients Mr Mudie and his middle-class readers
looked for. Shy heroines fell in love, passed through
suffering and sacrifice and finally with great patience and
piety won their happiness, or on the slightest deviation
from virtue ended in death and disaster.

Charlotte M. Yonge supplied Mr Mudie and his
subscribers with exactly what they wanted. Encouraged
to write by her neighbour John Keble, author of *The
Christian Year* and joint leader with Pusey and Newman
of the Oxford Movement, she published *The Heir of
Redclyffe* in 1853 when she was thirty and it immediately
became a best-seller. Mr Gladstone wept over the book
and Sir Guy Morville, the edifying hero, 'right-minded,
very well-informed and noble to a degree', not only
represented the ideal of all the idle young women waiting
for a husband, but of young men like William Morris,
Burne-Jones and Rossetti, who saw in this paragon of
virtue the spirit of a modern Crusader, which was
exactly what his author had intended. She had, in fact,
'fallen headlong in love with religion' at the age of twelve
and, sitting at the feet of Keble at Hursley parsonage, had
imbibed his strict Tractarian teaching with an enthusiasm
that remained with her for the rest of her long life.

Her career as a writer had thus begun and was continued with a serious purpose in mind—to make good-
ness attractive. And in book after book she succeeded in
conveying to her readers her own pleasure in the disci-
plined and devout family life of her characters, describing
the church bazaars and garden parties, games of croquet
and interior domestic scenes of home and rectory with a
fidelity born of familiarity and nourished on her High
Church principles. 'Miss Yonge's work,' as one critic
wrote, 'can with perfect propriety be left open on the
drawing-room table'—and Miss Yonge's own quiet way

of life with her father and mother at Otterbourne in Hampshire had the same perfect propriety. The Kebles at Hursley and Dr Moberly's large family of boys and girls at Winchester were her most dear and intimate friends. She had no need of others and was quite unspoilt by her fame; and because her father thought it would be unladylike for her to accept money for her work, she gave all her royalties away to the church and to Bishop Selwyn for his missionary schooner, the *Southern Cross*.

Mrs Henry Wood, Mrs Oliphant and Miss Braddon, the circulating library queens of the sixties, were less fastidious about their profits. Unlike Miss Yonge, who remained a spinster and could well afford to keep a carriage, they had to write to support themselves and their families. They added melodrama to the mixture of sentimentality, suffering and pious feeling, and gave their readers a thrilling sense of involvement with an upper-class world of sinful passion. Miss Braddon's *Lady Audley's Secret* caused a furore. Queen Victoria read it and admired it, and even those who were shocked by its hard-bitten heroine conceded that the book was not unfit for the young, since all through it 'vice is never sugared and no page, no sentence tempts youthful readers to lift the hidden veil'.

Miss Braddon, however, was soon out-distanced by a new authoress, Ouida, whose first novel *Held in Bondage* appeared in 1863 and at once started a new vogue in popular fiction, more daring and exotic than anything so far accepted by Mr Mudie. In fact, Mr Mudie was in a fix; by the time Ouida had written her fifth novel called *Under Two Flags*, the demand for her work was so great he simply could not refuse to circulate it, though he was aware that it deliberately flouted all the cherished virtues of Victorian respectability and revealed a flamboyant wickedness and seductiveness in 'High Life' that lifted his middle-class subscribers into a new and dangerously shocking vortex of pleasure. Ouida did not go in for veils. She could not be left open on the drawing-room table.

Born Louise Ramé in Bury St Edmunds of a mysterious French refugee who disappeared, and a middle-class English mother, she had never been able to pronounce her first name and had called herself Ouida as a child; and it was thus she signed the first stories she sent off to Harrison Ainsworth, the editor of *Bentley's Miscellany*. They were readable, exciting and imaginative. What she did not know she made up, writing at a furious pace and with great vivacity of places she had never seen and people she had never encountered. Her guardsmen were 'splendidly handsome, super-humanly strong and gifted', and her raven-haired heroines so beautiful they sacrificed virtue to passion without a qualm of conscience. Even the names of her characters—the Duchess of Margolds-warzel, the Marchioness of Margueterie and the Countess of Ormolu—had a reckless ring about them as they entered the fantastic world of her imagination, wearing white water-lilies in their hair or magnificent 'in some geranium-hued dress, as light and brilliant as summer clouds with the rose tint of sunset on them'. And as for the Hon. Bertie Cecil of the 1st Life Guards, known in the Brigade as 'Beauty', he lived in a brilliant whirl of luxury. 'Women sent him pretty things. . . . His dressing-table was littered with Bohemian glass and gold-stop-pered bottles, and all the perfumes of Araby represented by Breidenbach and Rimmel. His dressing-case was of silver with the name studded on the lid in turquoise; the brushes, boot-jacks, boot-trees, whipstands of ivory and tortoiseshell. . . . The hangings of the room were silken and rose-coloured, and a delicious confusion prevailed through it pell-mell—box spurs, hunting stirrups, cart-ridge cases, curb-chains, muzzle-loaders, hunting flasks, and white gauntlets being mixed up with Paris novels, pink notes, point-lace ties, bracelets and bouquets to be dispatched to various destinations, and velvet and silk bags for bank notes, cigars and vesuvians, embroidered by feminine fingers as useless as those pretty fingers themselves.' When the Hon. Bertie himself was revealed in this setting, 'on the softest of sofas, half dressed and having half an hour before plashed like a water dog out of a bath as big as a small pond . . . handsome, thoro'bred, languid, nonchalant and with a certain latent recklessness under the impassive calm of habit', it was not surprising if some of the feminine readers of this novel reached for their smelling-salts or, when disturbed by anyone, hid the book under a cushion.

Being the exact opposite of Charlotte M. Yonge, success went to Ouida's head and as soon as she became rich she began to live in the luxurious style she had created for her characters, without realizing that the glamorous world of her imagination was an illusion and that her own personal appearance failed entirely to match up to the brilliance and the beauty of her heroines. She took rooms for herself and her mother and her large New-foundland dog Sulla at the Langham Hotel, filled them with expensive and exotic flowers and ordered all her clothes from Worth in Paris. Then, dressed in white satin and enthroned on a red silk chair, with her mother in black lace as a foil and a duenna, she started giving even-ing parties for officers of the Guards and eminent men like Richard Burton, Bulwer Lytton and Sir Alexander Duff Gordon. Ladies, with the exception of Isabel Burton, were excluded from these gay assemblies in order that the gentlemen might smoke and drink and let themselves go in their conversation, and, perhaps, because Ouida did not like feminine competition. She believed she was a genius worthy of the highest admiration and a *grande amoureuse* irresistible to the opposite sex; and for a time when she moved to Italy and leased a large villa in Florence, she thought she had achieved all her desires, for English society abroad accepted her and she fell passionately in love with a handsome Tuscan nobleman, the Marchese della Stufa.

At her villa she surrounded herself with innumerable dogs and gorgeous flowers and entertained the *élite* of Florence on little chocolate cakes, ice-creams, marrons-glacés and delicious pastries from Doney's in the Via Tornabuoni. In the mornings she worked at her cinque-cento Venetian writing-desk under two great golden eagles that had once belonged to Napoleon; later she drove out in a white satin upholstered carriage behind her fast Maremma ponies, Mascherino and Birichino, or took her paint-box into the hills, where the vines and the olives glistened in the sunlight. Living on his estate nearby, the Marchese was her constant companion. He was charming, and very distinguished, with any number of saints and heroes among his ancestors reaching back into the thirteenth century—and he was also a bachelor. Ouida saw no reason why he should not marry her, for she still had no knowledge of the world and no idea that his mistress Mrs Ross, a high-born Englishwoman and the daughter of her friend Sir Alexander Duff Gordon, would prove such a formidable rival. The anguish of her awakening was for once entirely real; but when she saw her pleasure vanishing from her grasp, she did a fatal thing—she wrote the whole story very thinly disguised in her next novel *Friendship*, and was astonished when it gave offence to all her friends in Florence, besides making her look ridiculous.

Her readers in England, unaware of the real life drama going on in Italy, continued to enjoy her romantic fiction and were furious with Mr Mudie when he threatened to withdraw *Moths* from circulation on moral grounds. But after 1885, Ouida's popularity began to decline and her earnings no longer kept pace with her extravagance. Most of her former friends deserted her, and by 1893 she had moved to a large and dilapidated villa at Bellosguardo. 'There were only two or three chairs in the many rooms I traversed,' wrote Lady Paget after visiting her. 'A pink and gold paper hung in rags from the wall, there were no fires, no carpets. A troupe of fluffy and rather dirty white dogs barked at me and then rolled themselves under Ouida's feet, amongst the folds of a draggled black lace skirt. She wore a mantelet of some once bright but now faded colour, out of which her arms and tiny but ugly hands protruded. Her legs were encased in very bright blue stockings, and her feet in very thin white slippers.' And she evidently tried Lady Paget's loyalty to the utmost, for 'she insisted on walking through the lanes with me in this costume, with a whitey-browney hat with many feathers superadded and a spotty veil'.

Poor, foolish Ouida—having given so much pleasure to so many women with far less ability and courage than herself, she did not deserve her pitiful end. For a time she tried to supplement her income by turning to journalism, but her lurid style was not very suitable for any of the women's magazines then in circulation. These, like the long established *La Belle Assemblée* and the *Lady's Magazine*, combined fashion plates and sentimental romantic fiction with hints on the art of drawing and playing the piano and 'Familiar Lectures on Useful Sciences, such as Heraldry, Botany and Pneumatics'; and they were innocuous enough as a diversion. Yet a high-minded Wesleyan minister called Benjamin Gregory thought the *Lady's Magazine* was 'spiritually and practically unhealthful', since he believed 'it generated a taste for the kind of literary confectionary which could not nourish a robust fibre either of the mind or the heart'. Neither his mother nor his sister, both avid readers of the magazine, seem to have taken much notice of his strictures, and it is difficult to see how he could have objected to the 'Set of Rules and Maxims for Sweetening Matrimony' which appeared in one issue beside an instructive article on the 'Examination of a Mummy lately brought from Egypt'. If notice was also taken of 'the prettiest bonnets seen lately of straw-coloured riband ornamented with roses', even a Wesleyan minister should have known that nothing improves the moral fibre of a woman so much as a new bonnet.

No doubt Benjamin Gregory showed more approval of *Eliza Cook's Journal* which ignored fashion and other frivolous subjects altogether, the avowed purpose of the editress being 'to give her feeble aid to the gigantic struggle for intellectual elevation now going on' among the working classes. From the age of fifteen when her 'young bosom throbbed with rapture', Eliza Cook had been a prolific writer of verses, and when she launched her magazine she was still pouring out 'wild but earnest melodies from her soul' with absolute sincerity and a lofty desire to improve the minds of her readers. She published a large number of stories, or perhaps wrote them herself under the pseudonym of 'Silverpen', wherein the avarice and the haughtiness of rich were always overcome by the sufferings and the saintly example of the poor, and in a set of maxims headed 'Diamond Dust', likened bad temper to 'a Jar of Household Vinegar, in which all the Pearls of Happiness are dissolved'. Like Samuel Smiles's renowned book *Self Help*, Eliza Cook's somewhat doctrinaire opinions on how life should be lived appealed to the young women working long hours in the factories, who had scant leisure to enjoy anything and for the modest sum of one penny, swallowed her medicine whole for the sake of the thin sugar coating on the pill.

The fashion plates of *La Belle Assemblée* and the *Lady's Magazine* were aimed to give pleasure to the wives and daughters of the more well-to-do business men, living in the Victorian suburbs, who yearned to imitate the elaborate gowns worn in high society. By now the crinoline was so gigantic no well-dressed lady could get herself into a carriage or through a doorway without folding her skirts sideways on top of their huge wire cage. In a box at the opera or the theatre, there was very little room for her escort to do more than stand stiffly behind her to avoid crumpling the enormous frills and flounces of *mousseline-de-soie*, tarlatan and sarsenet that encircled her; and for day wear about the house she needed to move with care among the occasional tables loaded with the ornaments, flower vases, albums and fretted picture frames so dear to her Victorian heart.

Yet there was charm and grace in the crinoline style and a great deal of fine sewing. Quality and durability were highly prized. A best dress worn on Sundays one year might be unpicked at home and made over into a second best for the next year by the women who prided themselves on being economical. And in 1860 the exciting advent of cut out paper patterns in *The Englishwoman's Domestic Magazine* opened new horizons of pleasure to the more ambitious home dressmaker. Samuel Orchard Beeton, the editor, and his young wife Isabella, went off to Paris together on a very enjoyable business trip to taste the best in French cooking and to select a number of coloured fashion plates from the studio of M. Adolphe Goubaud for the novel idea they had thought up between them. Isabella, whose notes on cookery and household management had already appeared in the magazine as a preliminary to the publication of her famous book, had taste and a practical outlook. She knew exactly what would appeal to the women of Bayswater, Bromley and Birmingham and was clever enough to choose M. Goubaud's least *outré* designs as the first to be shown in *The Englishwoman's Domestic Magazine*. By sending '42 stamps', readers of the magazine could then

obtain a paper pattern of the published design together
with all the instructions on how to make their own
material up into a Parisian-looking gown.

The idea was a brilliant success. Sales of *The Englishwoman's Domestic Magazine* reached more than 50,000
copies a month; and in 1869 Mme Goubaud herself
settled in London, offering patterns 'tacked together and
trimmed' for a small additional charge, her list of desirable
garments including 'a Princess breakfast dress, A Veste
Russe for wearing under Zouave jackets, a Señorita
bodice and sleeve, a low Bodice for evening wear, lace
Pelerines, a Zerlina fichu, ladies' knickerbockers for
scarlet flannel and a summer Night-cap with strings.'
Any or all of these items indicate that home dressmaking
was no small undertaking; yet with the help of a sewing
woman and the new Singer sewing machine, the middle-
class housewife with enough leisure could make herself
look something like the opulent ladies she envied in the
class above her.

The fashionable silk mercers and linen drapers,
haberdashers and milliners had long since moved west-
wards from Covent Garden to Regent Street, Bond Street
and Oxford Street, but the pleasures of shopping had in
no way diminished since the days of Jane Austen's visit
to Layton & Shear's. The 'carriage trade' was still the aim
of the most exclusive shopkeepers, and Regent Street in
the season between two o'clock and four in the afternoon
was buzzing with 'the fireflies of fashion, glancing
rapidly hither and thither'. Smart carriages attended by
'gorgeously bedizened footmen', crawled through the
traffic of cabs, omnibuses, horsemen, pedestrians and
delivery vans in a scene of 'dizzying confusion'. Nash's
noble colonnade had been removed in 1848 as an 'improvement', at the instigation of a certain Mr Crane, a
hosier and glover, inventor and maker of the Patent Belt
Drawers; and in consequence of this act of vandalism,

the shops were able to increase in size and to display their goods behind huge plate-glass windows.

The Great Shawl and Clock Emporium of Farmer & Rogers claimed to be the largest and most celebrated of its kind in Europe and besides offering apparel 'of the most costly description for the carriage, promenade and opera', advertised, as a gesture towards the changing times, 'Shawls, cloaks and Dresses of First-class Taste and Quality at very Moderate Prices'. Mrs Addley Bourne of 37 Piccadilly, Family Draper, Jupon and Corset Manufacturer to the Court and Royal Family, went even further towards attracting the less aristocratic but prosperous middle-class trade to her exclusive salon. In 1866 she advertised 'A THOUSAND CRINOLINES AT HALF PRICE commencing at 5s 11d, usually 10s 6d. Piccadilly Puffed Jupons 15s 6d; striped Linsey 8s 3d. Beautiful shapes, but a little dusty'—a fact which no doubt did not deter the ladies who had the pleasure of snapping up such a bargain in puffed Jupons. They could also buy corsets, crinolines, camisoles and nightdresses named after royalty—the Alexandra corset, the Alice, Maude and Beatrice nightdresses—but never, of course, the unmentionable articles of underwear referred to as long-cloth drawers or knickerbockers. And although the omnibus made shopping easier and more pleasant for an infinite number of middle-class women, since it carried them into the West End without too much expense, they did not have to go there to buy what they wanted, for presently, like Mr Marshall and Mr Snelgrove and Mr Swan and Mr Edgar, Mr Derry amalgamated with Mr Toms in Kensington, Mr Barker opened a shop in the High Street and Mr William Whiteley, who proudly called himself the Universal Provider, established his shop in Bayswater.

Lace, ribbons, parasols, feather trimmings, Indian shawls, mantles and muffs were everywhere a temptation and a delight; even mourning apparel had its attractions according to the superior quality of the black crêpe used and the black jet bugles and beads decorating the widow's best dress of paramatta or cunningly disposed among the nodding black floriculture of her bonnet. For the trappings of grief and woe could be as fashionable as anything else, and women were the leaders of fashion now. Their husbands and brothers in the busy mid-Victorian world of getting and spending were doomed to the unrelieved monotony of the tall hat and the frock coat with here and there as a mark of distinction a fancy waistcoat or a frilled shirt. Gone were the Regency dandies—Brummell with his uninterrupted leisure, Alvanley and his debts, d'Orsay with his brilliance and his beauty; there remained only the ageing but elegant Disraeli. Long ago he had abandoned the green velvet trousers, canary-coloured waistcoats and buckled shoes he had worn in the salon of Lady Blessington—now he dressed in black as befitted the leader of the Conservative Party in the House of Commons. But his sable curls were as dark as ever on his pale brow, and it was his wife's pleasure to dye and cut his hair for him once a fortnight; after her death he discovered that she had kept every single curl she had ever cut from his head wrapped in small twists of tissue paper.

Disraeli's career was stranger and more romantic than any of the romantic novels he wrote and his marriage to Mary Anne the strangest episode of all. When he first met her she was the wife of Wyndham Lewis, Tory Member of Parliament for Maidstone—'a pretty little woman, a flirt and a rattle', thirteen years older than the melancholy young Hebrew with dark observant eyes, who became her protégé. Her influence, her money and her overwhelming desire to please him were useful—and more than useful when Wyndham Lewis died and she became an eligible widow with a house in Park Lane. But the unkind gossips who suggested he had wooed the widow for her money were wrong, and the people who laughed behind her back at her adoration of her beloved Dizzy, failed to judge her true character. Although a rattle to the end of her days and very eccentric in the way she got herself up in pink satin with diamond buttons and rivers of lace, to Disraeli she was ever 'the perfect wife', her good heart his refuge in times of stress, her gay, talkative enthusiasm his pleasure in times of prosperity. She understood him and she mothered him. When he came home from the House of Commons in the small hours of the morning, often tired and dispirited, she was there waiting for him, and wide awake with a roaring fire in the winter, bright lights and a good supper of game pie and champagne. Gradually he relaxed and unwound and told her everything that had happened in the House and her belief in him restored his confidence in himself as the dawn was breaking over Hyde Park.

But Disraeli did not achieve his ambition of becoming Prime Minister until 1867 and then only for a few months. His famous term of office came in 1874, by which time his lovable, eccentric and devoted Mary Anne was no longer alive to share his pride and he himself was a man of seventy. The supreme power he had longed for had come almost too late, yet the pleasure he gave the Queen was to crown his life with glory. The Queen disliked Mr Gladstone extremely. She complained that he spoke to her as if she were a public meeting; all his zeal, his punctilious attention to ceremony and his high-minded principles went for nothing, since he could not, or would not unbend with her or take his wife's advice 'to pet her a little'. Disraeli as a young man, intent upon the downfall of her favourite Minister Sir Robert Peel, had also earned Victoria's displeasure. Prince Albert had not approved of his unorthodox brilliance or of his gaudy waistcoats and his gold chains. But when Albert died, Disraeli's eulogies of the departed Prince persuaded the Queen that he alone was able to understand her grief. She wept over his letter of condolence and declared that he was the only person who appreciated the Prince; and when he wrote that his own acquaintance with the Prince had been 'one of the most satisfactory incidents of his life . . . full of refined and beautiful memories exercising over his remaining existence a soothing and exalting influence', she wept again at 'the depth and delicacy of his feelings.' At a touch of his magic lamp, the Oriental djinn not to be trusted with the affairs of the nation had turned into the friend and comforter of a lonely woman.

Thirteen years later when he became her Prime Minister for the second time with a large majority in the House of Commons, the Queen was overjoyed. She had never been more unpopular, nor had the English people been nearer to wishing for a republic. The monarchy was expensive and of what use, they asked, if the Queen never came out of the dull seclusion of her mourning to perform the ceremonial functions of the Crown? Where was the pageantry, the pleasure and the fun in having a Queen draped in weeping black crêpe, who moved sadly and alone from Windsor to Balmoral or to her island retreat at Osborne? It was true that Mr Gladstone had loyally defended her against the opprobrious Sir Charles Dilke and his republican rabble, but it was Disraeli who made her feel again the glory and the grandeur of her sovereign position.

He wooed her with exquisite flattery and he captured her heart and her imagination by appealing to all that was most colourful, emotional and repressed in her nature. After thirteen years of widowed gloom and frustration, she blossomed again at the age of fifty-five, like the primroses she picked at Osborne and sent to him in a moss-lined box with the royal coat of arms embossed on the lid. She became younger and prettier looking, those pouting lips in that round, obstinate face smiling and

chattering with a renewed gaiety that surpassed all ordinary intercourse between the Sovereign and her Minister.
Lord Melbourne had received her youthful affection,
Prince Albert her undying devotion, but only the fascinating, decaying old Jew with his gout and his asthma, his
dyed hair and his yellow face, by giving her reverence,
romance and a rapturous sense of her own imperial
majesty, could sweeten her middle years.

He persuaded her to reappear in public, to open
Parliament in person, to review her troops and distribute
medals at Aldershot, and the response of the people was
most gratifying. And, for six years in private audience with
her, through all the ups and downs of political strife, he
kept her enthralled. Writing to a friend from Osborne,
he said: 'I can only describe my reception by telling you
that I really thought she was going to embrace me. She
was wreathed with smiles and, as she tattled, glided about
the room like a bird.' Then he added significantly: 'We
are never so pleased as when we please others and, in our
gratified generosity, attribute to them the very results we
have achieved.' Thus the old oriental djinn laid his far-
flung achievements as a statesman at the feet of his 'Faery
Queen' and in doing so gave her the utmost satisfaction
as a woman and the English monarchy a prestige and a
popularity that were unique in the world. Thus he made
truth stranger and more romantic than fiction, and as he
lay dying at Hughenden with a bowl of the Queen's
primroses beside him, lived the last page of his own
romance from a dandified nobody to a Victorian Prime
Minister, an earldom and the Order of the Garter.

11
COUNTRY HOUSES, DONS
and
CURATES

THE WIDESPREAD POLITICAL and social changes of
the sixties and the seventies were slow in penetrating the
country-side, chiefly because the highest aim of the
successful self-made banker or business man was to buy
an estate in the shires and become one of the landed
gentry. Disraeli himself, in his fight for recognition in the
Tory party, had bought the manor of Hughenden in
Buckinghamshire on money borrowed from Lord George
Bentinck, and several members of the fabulous Rothschild
family, grandsons of a Jew Street pedlar in Frankfurt,

were his near neighbours. There was Baron Lionel who advanced the four million sterling Disraeli needed for his Suez Canal coup, with three thousand five hundred acres of land at Tring and the seventeenth-century manor house which had once been the home of Nell Gwynn. Then there were Lionel's two brothers, Anthony at Aston Clinton near Aylesbury and Meyer at Mentmore Towers, a luxurious Anglo-Norman castellated mansion designed for him by Paxton and surrounded by groves of trees, rich pastures, racing stables and a stud farm. 'The Medicis were never lodged so in the height of their glory,' was Lady Eastlake's comment on Mentmore Towers, where the hunting, the shooting and the garden fêtes, the carriage drives and the Lucullan picnics of lobster mousse, paté, soufflés and champagne provided a continuous round of bucolic pleasure in the lush green beauty of the English countryside.

And not very far away, there was Ferdinand, an Austrian cousin of Lionel and his brothers, who began building Waddesdon Manor in 1874, a gigantic pile of stone copied from the Châteaux of the Loire and featuring the towers of Maintenon, the chimneys of Chambord and the staircases of Blois in the midst of Buckinghamshire. To achieve his purpose he sliced off the top of a hill and had it levelled down to sustain his colossal mansion; then he transplanted thousands of large trees and shrubs to the vicinity, bought fountains, peacocks and statuary to adorn his terraced walks, imported hundreds of tropical birds for his aviary and built glasshouses of a mile or more in extent to provide him with peaches, nectarines and muscat grapes, arum lilies and orchids at all seasons of the year. Indoors there were 222 rooms richly decorated with panelling, paintings, marbled floors and carved ceilings, with Louis Quinze and Louis Seize gilt furniture, Sèvres china, Savonnerie carpets, embroidered curtains, Beauvais tapestries and *objets d'art* of every conceivable sort and size from the smallest Fabergé snuff-box to an outsize musical elephant. Never since the days of the Regent had money been lavished with more extravagance on the personal pleasure of an individual—but with a difference, since money with the Rothschilds never ran out, it flowed like a splendid river of liquid gold.

Subtle as their oriental forefathers and united as a family, they bought their way into English society with a shrewd and calculating brilliance. Natty, Leo and Alfred, the charming sons of Baron Lionel, and Ferdinand himself, became such close friends of the Prince of Wales that before long it was not the hereditary peers of England whose names appeared continually in the Court Circular from Marlborough House, but the Rothschilds'. *Nouveaux-riches* or not, their society was the gayest, the most amusing and the most sought after in the smart set revolving round the Prince of Wales. They went racing, hunting, shooting and yachting in the English manner and gave magnificent parties, where it was nothing for the ladies to find some exquisite jewelled ornament wrapped in the lace napkin beside their places at the dinner-table. Their chefs were the finest and the most celebrated in the world and every meal they served was a banquet. No Rothschild ever grudged a single guinea he spent on the entertainment of his friends and to be a guest from Saturday to Monday at one of their establishments was to enjoy the art of living in the grand manner.

Naturally some of the county families of aristocratic origin did not approve of the Rothschilds or of the invasion of the shires by the rich industrialists so eager to become landowners and gentlemen. Yet as time went on the new men were gradually absorbed into country society. They sent their sons to the public schools in the south of England and endeavoured to marry their daughters off with a handsome dowry to any impoverished young gentleman of the aristocracy or the squirearchy who would take them on. They built alms-houses and schools in the village, refurbished the ancient churches and spent their money freely on local entertainment. They kept horses and carriages and innumerable servants and did their best to conform to the ways of the gentry. And they also took immense trouble to 'improve' their houses, adding Victorian turrets and fretted Gothic features to the harmonious exterior of many a Georgian mansion, besides indulging in all the modern comforts money could buy.

Indeed the comfort of English country houses, whether they belonged to the parvenu industrialists or to the established gentry, surprised and delighted visitors from abroad. Fanny Kemble, the actress daughter of Charles Kemble, after her disastrous marriage to an American and her unhappy attempt to live on his plantation in the South, on returning to England went to visit Lord and Lady Dacre at the Hoo, an old house near Hitchin. 'I love the country for itself,' she wrote, 'and the species of life which combines as these people lead it, the pleasure of the highest civilization with the wholesome enjoyment nature abounds in, seems to me the perfection of existence.' She enjoyed the long country walks, the visits to church on Sunday mornings with the whole family, 'the amiable and pleasant company' and the charming English landscape. The contrast with American life as she had seen it was profound.

Comparisons between the two countries did not, however, always end in England's favour. Ellen Dwight of Boston, who married the Hon Edward Twisleton and was taken by him to visit his relations at Adlestrop and Stoneleigh, asserted that 'among all the luxury and splendour of England our American simplicity of life loses nothing in my estimation'. None the less she was deeply impressed by the immense four-posters, the immense wardrobes and wash-stands in the bedrooms, 'with chintz curtains to the bed and windows and a small sofa covered with the same . . . all the perfection of comfort': and this comfort maintained by a large staff of servants whose business it was to carry a never-ending chain of brass and copper cans of hot water upstairs to fill the immense wash-stands and the baths set in front of the fire in winter for the pleasure of the guests. At Stoneleigh there was a ball with country dances that amused everyone, and a fashionable archery meeting where the ladies wore special kid boots with cork soles to protect them from any ill-effects they might suffer from standing on the damp grass. At Adlestrop everything was of the utmost elegance with 'a complete silver service, with dish covers and all, and silver handles to the knives', and also 'a new set of china for breakfast about every other day, with a little sugar-bowl and cream-jug for each person'.

Breakfast was an informal meal—everyone helped themselves from the array of hot dishes on the sideboard; and by the seventies, when Richard Henry Dana, a Harvard undergraduate, came to England, afternoon tea had become fashionable. He found it 'very refreshing, the tea very hot, the bread and butter very thin and the small sugared cakes delicious'. Coming from a cultured American family with the correct letters of introduction, his entrée into the best society was assured and he marvelled at the way 'the English have carried hospitality to a fine art'. Compared with America where 'a three days' visit is a burden', he wrote, 'since the host and hostess always over-entertained their guests and no one was given a moment's leisure or quiet', the freedom of hospitality in English society was unique—'that is, among themselves and to anyone who is properly introduced', he added, accepting the exclusiveness as well as the liberal generosity of the aristocracy without question. Having once forgotten his father's advice not to address anyone as my lord duke or my lady duchess, he noticed that the Countess of Althorp 'fairly cringed' every time he used her title and he never made the same mistake again.

Dana visited Oxford and found the same kind of hospitality there—a respect for the individual and his own way of enjoying himself. He was invited to breakfast by a scholar at Balliol who scrambled his own eggs on the fire and made the tea and toast, had dinner in Hall at Christ Church and luncheon with Matthew Arnold's son. The river and the meadows and the college boat races, the splendid lawns and the quiet gaieties of the evening with good conversation and much debating, music and the mid-summer balls all gave him great pleasure. The whole atmosphere he thought was 'more blithe and jovial than at Harvard where men took both work and play more seriously', and he never forgot the kindness he received from everyone.

Learning and leisure were graciously combined in the tranquil surroundings of the University for those who were fortunate enough to work there. But it was with more than a twinge of the mid-Victorian guilty conscience that C. L. Dodgson, the thirty-one-year-old mathematical tutor at Christ Church, wrote in his diary for December 1863: 'Here, at the close of another year, how much of neglect, carelessness and sin have I to remember! I had hoped, during the year, to have made a beginning in parochial work, to have thrown off habits of evil, to have advanced in my work at Christ Church. How little, next to nothing has been done of all this! Now I have a fresh year before me; once more let me set myself to do something worthy of life "before I go hence and be no more seen. . . ." ' He could not know that his worthy aspirations to do something good with his life would be quite forgotten by posterity while the more frivolous pursuits of his leisure would one day make the name of Lewis Carroll immortal—for it was to amuse three small daughters of the Dean of Christ Church, Lorina, Alice and Edith Liddell, that he first invented the story of *Alice's Adventures in Wonderland,* one summer afternoon when he took them up the river to Godstow.

'Mr Dodgson always wore black clergyman's clothes in Oxford,' Alice recorded in later life, 'but when he took us on the river, he used to wear white flannel trousers. He also replaced his black top-hat with a hard white straw hat on these occasions, but of course retained his black boots, because in those days white tennis shoes had never been heard of. He always carried himself upright, almost more than upright, as if he had swallowed a poker.' He was not, however, in the least unbending with his young friends; they adored his fantastical jokes and stories, and it was Alice, his favourite, who begged him to write them down for her. These days, or when it was too wet to picnic up the river and the children came to his rooms and sat on the sofa beside him while he entertained them, were the happiest he had ever known and marked with 'a white stone' in his diary. But it was rather a shock to him when he discovered that Mrs Liddell did not quite approve of the pleasure he took in amusing her little girls. It was even suggested at one time that he was chasing the governess, Miss Prickett, though nothing could have been farther from the truth for women scared this shy and imaginative clerical don with a stammer and it was only in the society of very young children that he found his true affinity. Alice, besides, was the most perfect model for the hobby that appealed to him more than any other and he never tired of posing her in front of his camera.

Photography was not entirely new; it had been developed in the thirties and the forties by Henry Fox Talbot in England and by Louis Daguerre in France. But Dodgson was one of the first amateurs to realize its possibilities as an art and to enjoy experimenting with all the paraphernalia and the patience that the cumbersome cameras of his day demanded. 'Bought some collodion at Telfer's and spent the morning at the Deanery. . . . The two dear little girls Ina and Alice were with me all the morning. . .'; this day also was marked with a white stone in his diary as were many others when Alice with her big, innocent eyes and her fey expression, posed for him in her best silk dress and her smart little button boots, or barefoot as a beggar child against the sun-dappled wall of the Deanery garden. Unhappily it never occurred to Dodgson that little girls grow into bigger girls, or if it did occur to him, he found it difficult to accept, and by the time Alice had reached her twelfth year, relations with the Deanery had become desperately strained. 'During these last few days,' he wrote, 'I have applied in vain to take the children on the river, i.e. Alice, Edith and Rhoda; but Mrs Liddell will not let *any* come in future— rather superfluous caution,' he added in a fury of bitterness and frustration, for however equivocal his own position might appear, it annoyed him to see his young friends deprived of their fun.

Other mothers besides Mrs Liddell sometimes showed the same reluctance in allowing their little girls to visit Dodgson, but the children themselves were fascinated by his society and he continued to collect them round him like a bunch of rosebuds. Ethel Arnold, who knew him in the seventies, wrote afterwards: 'It was no joke being photographed in those days, and for a nervous child, dressed up as a Heathen Chinese or a fisher-maiden, to keep still for 45 seconds at a time was no mean ordeal. . . . But I never catch a whiff of the potent odour of collodion nowadays without instantly being transported on magic wings of memory to Lewis Carroll's dark-room, where, shrunk to childhood's proportions, I see myself watching open-mouthed the mysterious process of coating the plate, or, standing on a box drawn out from under the sink to assist my small dimensions, watching the still more mysterious process of development. And the stories! The never-ending, never-failing stories he told in answer to our never-ending demands! He was indeed a bringer of delight in those dim far-off days, and I look back on the hours spent in his dear, much-beloved company as an oasis of brightness in a somewhat grey and melancholy childhood.'

Dodgson's skill as a photographer brought him into contact with Rossetti, Millais, Burne-Jones and other artists, whose sympathy stimulated his interest in the visual arts. On his visits to London, staying quietly at the old Hummums Hotel in Covent Garden, he never missed an opportunity of going to the Royal Academy, then at the height of its glory as the acknowledged arbiter of taste in Victorian painting, or to the exhibitions of the Royal Photographic Society; and he was a keen theatre-goer, enraptured by the ravishing freshness of the fifteen-year-old Ellen Terry and her sister Kate. One morning he put all his camera equipment in a cab and drove to the Terrys and spent the whole day taking pictures of the girls—a day marked with another white stone in his diary. Ellen, he thought, was 'lively and pleasant, almost childish in her fun, but perfectly lady-like'—an attribute which appealed not only to Dodgson, but to G. F. Watts, the painter, who admired the mystical and medieval beauty he saw in her and within a year had married her.

Watts lived *en prince* in a studio in the garden of Little Holland House, the home of his mother Mrs Thoby Prinsep, the most formidable of the Pattle sisters and the most determined celebrity hunter in London. Pampered and spoilt by a court of adoring middle-aged women who enjoyed submitting to his slightest whim, he was more than twice the age of his child bride and of a bilious temper. But Ellen at first was bright-eyed at the thought of living in this 'artistic' environment and quite innocent of the fact that her irrepressible spirits and childish fun would be entirely at odds with the atmosphere of holy worship surrounding her querulous husband. In later life she generously absolved Watts himself of any guilt in abruptly getting rid of her after a few months of wedlock, though at the time she was mortified and felt very miserable. The ladies at Little Holland House hushed up the affair, arranged a separation and drew a veil over the whole episode, while poor Ellen was sent home to her family in disgrace and went back to the theatre. Nothing remained of her brief association with Watts except his idealized, soulful portraits of her and the photographs taken by Mrs Prinsep's domineering sister, Julia Margaret Cameron.

This strange and eccentric Victorian lady was even more obsessed than Dodgson by the new art of the camera. She took up photography at the age of fifty in a fit of domestic idleness and depression while her husband and her sons were away in India, and pursued her pleasure with a farouche intensity that often embarrassed her friends. At Little Holland House she met all the literary and artistic lions of the day, and few of them ever succeeded in escaping the ordeal of sitting in front of her magic black box. She was determined to record faithfully 'the greatness of the inner as well as the features of the outer man', and she succeeded brilliantly with her portraits of Carlyle, Darwin and Tennyson. But for Tennyson she conceived an admiration so excessive that when she moved to Freshwater on the Isle of White to be near him, he sometimes found her devotion troublesome. She showered him with generous though often unwelcome gifts, once arriving on his doorstep with two legs of Welsh mutton, and another time staggering under a load of blue wallpaper embossed with a frieze copied from the Elgin Marbles, and she wrote long, romantic letters to him, pestering him to come and sit for his portrait.

Having turned her coal-cellar at Freshwater into a dark-room and a glazed chicken-house in the garden into a studio, her enthusiasm for photography became an absolute mania. If her distinguished friends were not available, she draped her long-suffering parlourmaid as an angel or in some Pre-Raphaelite pose of melancholy womanhood, or if she saw a good-looking stranger in the street, inveigled him into her chicken-house and kept him there for the afternoon. Meals were forgotten or set aside even when guests were staying in the house; and when at last she had created a successful picture, she would come running into the dining-room in triumph like Lady Macbeth, with the crimson and violet draperies she wore flowing out behind her and her face and hands stained with chemicals, flourishing a wet photographic plate that dripped all over the carpet and left indelible marks on the table napery. Nothing was allowed to come between her and the pursuit of her ideal, and although Dodgson criticized her work for its technical imperfections, she did achieve astonishing results in her portrait studies, which revealed the character of her sitters in a remarkable way. She was less happy with the outsize allegorical compositions she designed to illustrate Tennyson's poems, with the porter from Yarmouth Pier dressed up as King Arthur, and caused the poet some consternation when her visual ideas did not tally with his own, but her adoration of him never wavered and there was little he could do to protect himself from her persistence.

Tennyson had settled at Farringford three years after his marriage at the age of forty-one to Emily Sellwood. 'The peace of God entered into my life after I married her,' he declared, and in this wonderful year of 1850 when he married Emily and published *In Memoriam*, he at last found fulfilment. All the grief and the loneliness he had suffered since the death of his dear friend Arthur Hallam, all the disappointment he had known as a poet whose genius was misunderstood, and all the anguish of his young manhood with a drunken, clerical father, a gentle, adoring mother and a large number of temperamental brothers and sisters for whom he felt responsible—all these distorted and tangled ends of distress were suddenly, miraculously woven into a new pattern of calm and glad acceptance. With his appointment as Poet Laureate on the death of Wordsworth, his whole future was assured. Friends still noticed the fire and the melancholy in his dark eyes, but his rugged features, so full of power, passion and intellect, so strong, dark and impressive, now wore a more tranquil expression, and his dear Emily, a woman of rare and beautiful understanding whom he had loved when he was ten years younger and unable to support a wife, did her best to shield his abnormal sensitivity from the pin-pricks of daily life.

He was pathologically shy and awkward in society, except in the company of his intimate friends, and he retired to Farringford to escape the trivial demands of the people who sought aquaintance with him now that he was famous; such people, he thought, treated great men 'like pigs to be ripped open for the public'. Farringford was secluded, the house situated in a small park of its own and surrounded by beautiful unspoilt country, where the birds and the butterflies hovered above the wild flowers and the sweet-smelling thyme in the downland grass and, less than a mile away, the chalk cliffs met the restless, ever-changing sea. Here Tennyson found a pleasure he had never known before. He could work and meditate without being worried by intruders, watch over his two boys and go for long walks over the downs with the wind in his hair and his head in the skies. He never got tired of looking at the landscape or of working in his garden, and one morning Dodgson, on a visit to Freshwater, walked over to Farringford and found him in a wide-awake hat and spectacles, mowing his lawn with evident delight. He was so myopic he did not at once recognize his visitor, but on doing so, welcomed him most warmly and took him into the house and up into his study where they talked for two hours on the conflict between science and religion that so disturbed the minds of their contemporaries and themselves. Mrs Tennyson had been ill and was lying on the sofa downstairs; even so she invited Dodgson to dinner the next evening and he enjoyed himself immensely, again retiring to the study to talk for another two hours. Tennyson walked back through the garden with his guest and Dodgson marvelled at his observation when, looking up at the moon, he pointed out the ring of light round it which he had described in one of his early poems:

> Like the tender amber round
> Which the moon about her spreadeth
> Moving through a fleecy night.

It was partly this exact observation of nature and his power of describing what he saw in the most mellifluous language that made Tennyson the favourite poet of a whole generation. Men and women were carried away by the surging sound of his poetry, the melancholy, autumnal beauty of his elegiac phrases and his high idealism. Francis Kilvert, the young curate at Clyro in Radnorshire and later of his father's parish near Chippenham, wept over *In Memoriam* and, when he went to call on a sick child, tried to soothe her by reading aloud *The May Queen* and *The Miller's Daughter*. The child fell asleep, which was no criticism of the poet's inspiration but the whole point of the curate's kindly ministrations to her need. For Kilvert was blessed with a very kind heart. In many ways—in his sentimentality, his self-questioning, his piety and his respectability—he was a typical product of the mid-nineteenth century environment. Yet for a

Victorian clergyman he was extraordinarily free from humbug and narrow-minded doctrinaire opinion; and he endeared himself so much to the people of Clyro that when he left the parish after seven years among them, the school children saved up their pennies to buy him a gold pencil case to hang on his watchchain, the vicar gave him 'a magnificent writing desk of Coromandel wood bound with brass, fitted with polished Mahogany and containing two most secret drawers' and the three Miss Baskervilles, daughters of the squire at Clyro Court, presented him with a travelling bag. 'What have I done? What am I that these people should so care for me?' he asked, adding with a genuine humility: 'How little I have deserved it. Lord requite these people ten thousandfold into their bosom, the kindness they have showed to a stranger.' And, preaching a farewell sermon on his last Sunday, he was so overcome he burst into tears in the pulpit.

'Every tree and hill and hollow and glimpse of the mountains' was precious to him as he went about his Christian mission in the countryside, and at all seasons of the year he took pleasure in the landscape, recording his delight in page after page of his diary. 'The whole country is now lighted up by the snowy pear blossoms among their delicate light-green leaves. The pear trees stand like lights about the gardens and orchards and in the fields. . . .' 'A heavenly day, reminding one of Wordsworth's *March Noon*, larks mounting, bees humming, lambs playing, children in the lanes gathering violets and primroses and the mountains streaked and striped and ribbed with snow. . . .' 'This afternoon I walked over to Lanhill. As I came down from the hill into the valley across the golden meadows and along the flower-scented hedges a great wave of emotion and happiness stirred and rose up in me. I know not why I was so happy, nor what I was expecting, but I was in a delirium of joy, it was one of those supreme few moments of existence, a deep delicious draught from the strong sweet cup of life. . . .' Thus in marvellous detail and with a poetic eye, he noted everything down. Two men fishing on the lake at Bowood in Wiltshire and 'a coot skimming along the surface with a loud cry and a rippling splash'; buying a new pair of elastic boots with gutta-percha soles in Salisbury and seeing a collection of stuffed birds in the vicar's house at Britford; gathering nuts in Seagry woods with a party of children 'amidst shouts and screams of laughter', or skating on the ice by torchlight to the sound of a quadrille band among the gentry at Draycott. 'Why do I keep this voluminous journal?' he once asked himself. 'Partly because life appears to me such a curious and wonderful thing that it almost seems a pity that even such a humble and uneventful life as mine should pass away without some such record as this.'

No one ever enjoyed the simple pleasures of the country more than Kilvert. He got up at six in the morning on Easter Sunday to gather primroses, went for long, solitary walks in the mountains or drove in the vicar's dogcart to dine with Mrs Bevan and 'the dear girls' at Hay Castle. There were picnics, archery meetings and dances with claret cup and parsnip wine; penny readings for the poor in the villages, church fêtes and garden parties; tea parties and tennis; an eclipse of the moon, balloon ascents and a panorama by magic lantern of Dr Livingstone exploring Africa—all to make life a most curious and wonderful thing. And there were the girls—an endless number of pretty girls, everywhere he went and all round him; pretty girls of all ages—in school, on the farms, at the Manor House. Young girls to 'romp' with, older girls with sweet blue eyes, pearly teeth, tossing curls, mischievous glances, rounded arms 'as creamy as the milk' and white bosoms 'heaving tenderly'.

Girls bewitched this sensitive and sentimental curate

and sent him into ecstasies. Gypsy Lizzie in his reading class at school, with her unsuspecting innocence and dark soft curls—'Oh, child, child, if you did but know your own power! Oh, Gypsy, if you only grow up as good as you are fair!' Lovely Florence Hill 'opening her blue eyes wide with a sweet, surprised look peculiar to herself . . . and a quick, timid, almost breathless way of speaking . . . beautiful and wild and stately, a true mountain child.' Dear little Janet in bed 'pretty and rosy with tumbled curly hair, who soon had her round plump limbs out from under the sheets with the innocent simplicity of child-hood and her pretty little white feet in my lap.' And sweet Daisy Thomas who came into the drawing-room, 'shy, confused and blushing painfully', then took him into the garden where she picked him a sprig of 'sweet-scented verbena'—or at a croquet party 'in a black velevet jacket and light dress, with a white feather in her hat and her bright golden hair tied up with blue riband. How bright and fresh and happy and pretty she looked. . . . Oh, Daisy. . .!'

Kilvert actually went to Daisy's father, feeling 'fright-fully nervous' and boldly announced 'I am attached to one of your daughters', but as he only had one sovereign in the world at that moment, Mr Thomas seemed 'a good deal taken aback' and Daisy was given 'a hint not to be too forthcoming'. To forget her seemed impossible; Kilvert dried the flowers of the nosegay she had once given him and pressed them in his album, grieving sadly for his lost love. Then, once again, at a wedding party near Worthing, he was overcome by a new face: sweet Katie, 'a tall handsome girl with very dark hair, eyebrows and eyelashes and beautiful bright grey eyes', and again he lost his heart as they sat on the downs talking and gazing into each other's eyes. But Katie was not to be his wife either. Kilvert was thirty-nine and the vicar of Bredwardine on the Wye before he met and married

Elizabeth Anne Rowland—and five weeks later he died suddenly of peritonitis. The life that had seemed such a curious and wonderful thing was over. There were no more pleasant walks in the mountains, no more gay and delightful games of croquet and no more girls—there was only the still more wonderful hope of a new life in eternity 'among the birds and flowers of Paradise'.

12

FUN

and

FROLIC

THE SOCIALLY INEPT curate and the parson—or the parson's wife—were a familiar amusement to the readers of *Punch*, always depicted in some awkward situation and suffering from acute shyness. Yet it was they and the Nonconformist ministers in the towns and cities who endeavoured to find some alternative to the gin palace, the beer shop and the 'penny gaff' for the raffish, under-nourished dregs of society. It might be the pleasure of saving their souls, of persuading them to deny themselves strong liquor altogether and to join the Temperance Movement, or it might be the pleasure of improving their minds with lectures and demonstrations and sometimes giving the children a day out in the country. Whatever turn of benevolence the interference of the clergy took, it was inspired by a worthy motive which spread very slowly into the minds of the upper classes; for while millions of pounds were subscribed by them in overseas missions to the heathen to save his black soul from the devil, very little notice was taken of the utter squalor and degradation industrialism had bred at home—or not until the seventies, when Miss Octavia Hill's reforming zeal began to attract attention and it became the fashion for young ladies of leisure in society to go 'slumming' in the East End of London, dressed, of course, to meet the occasion in washable kid gloves and sensible shoes.

Some were sincere and some were not. Kate Potter and her sister Beatrice, the future Mrs Sidney Webb, believed in what they were doing and discovered a new faith which was to lead Beatrice into the Fabian Society and her life-long devotion to Socialism. Miss Henrietta Rowland came from a similar background. She was young, attractive and rich, 'with brown curls down her back, handsome furs and a fashionable Tyrolese hat'—and the last thing she ever intended to do was to marry Samuel Barnett, the unpreposessing son of an iron-bedstead maker who was a curate at Bethnal Green. Yet his strength and his humility, his courage and his devotion quite overcame her embarrassment at the sight of his black cotton gloves which were always too large and his battered silk hat which was always too small; and, having married him, she discarded her furs and settled into the gloomy vicarage of St Jude's, Whitechapel, where there was no bathroom or pantry and the windows looked out on a grey street leading to a red-brick slaughterhouse.

Mrs Barnett did not complain. She started by brightening the vicarage up with chintz curtains, wax fruit and stuffed birds under glass, and she proved to be the perfect wife for this original and imaginative Victorian parson. Together they set about organizing the pleasure of their wretched, poverty-stricken parishioners—and succeeded brilliantly, because they brought gaiety and colour into the lives of many whose whole experience was limited to the rookery of crowded and insanitary

courts and alleys in the neighbourhood. Though often
charged with being unorthodox, since it was their idea
to reveal God through the works of man and by common
fellowship as much as in the sacraments of the Church,
they continued their work for thirty years with tireless
energy and a spirit of goodwill entirely free from self-
righteousness. 'I do not want much,' Canon Barnett
said. 'I should like the best things made free. . . baths and
wash-houses, specially swimming baths . . . books and
pictures . . . so that every man may have a public library
or a picture gallery as his drawing-room. Poverty cannot
pay for the pleasure which satisfies and yet, without the
pleasure the people perish.'

It was not often that the class structure of Victorian
England admitted such a deviation from the rules of what
was fit for the poor and what was not, and Canon
Barnett was criticized accordingly. Sermons and Sundays
loomed large in the lives of everyone, but man was not
equal in the sight of God and in church, as everywhere
else, the classes did not mix. Family pews were the
privilege of the rich; the rest of the congregation was
segregated from them. The morning parade after church
belonged to the ladies in fashionable bonnets and their
overdressed offspring carrying velvet-covered prayer
books and bibles, with the father of the family at the
head of the procession. It was enough if the servants were
let off to go to church in the evening, leaving but one
of them in to provide a cold supper. And, in the country,
the congregation stood up when the squire and his lady
arrived at the church door.

All through society there was the most complicated
code of distinction between one class and another and
books on etiquette were the best-sellers of the day, acting as a guide through the labyrinth for the snobs and
the social climbers. It was permissible to ask your doctor
to dinner but not his wife, to entertain the vicar at the

family table but to give the curate a glass of sherry and send him about his business. It was correct to keep the governess or the tutor upstairs when guests were expected in the drawing-room, and very incorrect for ladies to speak to gentlemen unless they had been formally introduced. Young girls were kept in the school-room until they were old enough to put their hair up and be chaperoned through their first season; boys who had failed in their studies or brought grief to their parents by their folly, were shipped off to Canada rather than endure the stigma of becoming *déclassé* in Britain. The lady of leisure dressed by a court dressmaker could not be confused with the woman who bought her clothes ready-made; the gentleman in his tall hat and frock-coat was distinct from the man who wore a bowler—and neither of them had anything to do with the cloth-cap wearers belonging to the amorphous mass of the unskilled and the illiterate. Only very seldom did people of all classes meet on the same footing—only on the race-course and then only on one day of the year—for the Derby.

This was the English equivalent of a carnival day on the Continent and the greatest leveller in Victorian society. In 1840 an American clergyman on a visit to England got caught up in the crowd at Epsom by mistake and described his experience in a letter to his parishioners at home. 'The first thing that particularly struck me,' he wrote, 'was the mixed character of the multitude. Kindred tastes had brought together, upon this great arena, the extremes of society and into the closest contact. Here were the carriages of the nobility, emblazoned with their appropriate coat of arms and attended by liveried footmen; and the cabs and carts in which not a few of the *ignobile vulgus* had been borne to the scene of dissipation. In the same throng, pressing forward to gaze upon the exciting spectacle, were the gentry and the very off-scouring of the earth, clad in rags and squalidness. In

the same group, or standing near each other, might have
been seen high born ladies, servant girls, gypsies and the
most worthless of the sex, all pressing forward in one
broad extended ring to witness the races. . . .'

None of all this, of course, gave pleasure to the rector
of St Andrew's Church, Philadelphia. 'How true it is,'
he went on, 'that all the unregenerate whatever may be
their circumstances in life possess kindred tastes, which
frequently bring them together here and will assuredly
place them in the same company and assign them to the
same doom in the future world! In the interval between
the races, the course ground was filled with rope-dancers,
jugglers, necromancers and various kinds of gamesters;
and on the outskirts of the course were fixed up long
lines of splendid booths and pavilions, which contained
the appliances and paraphernalia of gambling and carous-
ing on the most extended scale. . . . It seemed,' he concluded, 'as though there was here brought before me,
in one concentrated and panoramic view, an exhibition
of the world's varied allurements of sin.'

Perhaps it was impossible for an American clergyman
to appreciate the absolute hold on the English imagination of the Derby. The scene had not changed when
Frith painted it several years later. The very rich and the
very poor still shared the strong instinct for gambling
that had brought them together in the Regency; it was
only the middle classes, as guardians of the Noncomfor-
mist conscience, who disapproved of betting. Lord
Hastings lost £100,000 on the Derby in 1867, Lord
Chaplin won £20,000, and no amount of exhortation or
example had really succeeded in eradicating the ingrained
habit of those whom the Reverend John Clark called the
off-scouring of the earth. If they could not get to the
race-course they emptied their pockets of the little money
they had earned or stolen at cards and dice, shove-
h'apenny, chuck-farthing and pitch and toss in the pubs,

on doorsteps and in sleazy back rooms. Brawling and fighting were the natural outcome and a kind of fun unknown to the more genteel section of the community—the only fun for the *ignobile vulgus* for whom there was nothing between the penny reading or the pot house.

Organized games were the privilege of the public schools and the middle classes, not of the people below them, who were not expected to let off steam except on public holidays. And of the big annual fairs held in London at Easter and Whitsun, only Greenwich survived into the seventies, getting shabbier and more corrupt. The gaiety Dickens had found there in 1835, with everyone smoking and drinking and larking about in a perpetual bustle of noise and excitement, had degenerated into a disreputable orgy by the time Nathaniel Hawthorne went to the Fair in the late sixties. There were still oysters and whelks, toys and trinkets and gingerbread for sale, pickled salmon, pea-nuts and oranges, 'the withered ones boiled to give them a look of freshness'; and there was still Wombwell's menagerie of dusty lions and tired-looking elephants, the man monkey, and Toby the learned pig, who could 'spell, read, cast accounts, tell the points of the sun's rising and setting and the age of any party'. But the theatrical booths were not what they had been in the days of John Richardson, the famous travelling showman of the earlier years of the century. 'The actors,' wrote Hawthorne, 'were woefully shabby, with very dingy wrinkled white tights, threadbare cotton velvets, crumpled silk and crushed muslin, all the gloss and the glory gone out of their aspect and attire, seen thus in the broad daylight and after a long series of performances.'

The great days of the travelling showmen were over. People were getting about more themselves on the railways and could go farther afield for their entertainment on excursions to the country or the seaside. But balloon ascents from Greenwich Park and Cremorne Gardens were still a popular spectacle as they had been in the fifties, when Mrs Graham elected 'to share the perilous honours of the sky' with her husband, Mr Graham. Appropriately their first matrimonial ascent together was celebrated by the waving of hundreds of white satin flags. 'I need not say anything respecting Mrs Graham's behaviour on this occasion,' her husband wrote afterwards. 'Her conduct on entering the car was quite sufficient to prove the pleasure I experienced from her company and remarks on the voyage.' And even on another occasion when the balloon they were travelling in collided with a flagpole and finished up on the roof of Colonel North's house in Arlington Street, Mrs Graham kept her nerve and her conduct continued to please her admiring spouse, who disentangled her petticoats from the ropes and the chimney-pots and carried her down to safety.

Cremorne kept going as the last of the Pleasure Gardens and in the sixties was the haunt of Whistler and his friends. The gaieties included elaborate firework displays, cosmoramic pictures and a Stereorama, fun in the fernery and dancing on the open air crystal platform by the river. But, by the seventies, when that observant visitor from Paris, Hippolyte Taine, went there in search of amusement, the company had deteriorated. There was 'a crush and much shoving at the entrance', he remarked, 'and the press of people was dreadful, but it was possible to get a breath of fresh air in the darker corners. All the men are well or at least neatly dressed; the women prostitutes but of a higher rank than those in the Strand; light coloured shawls over white gauze or tulle dresses, red mantelets, new hats. Some of their dresses may have cost as much as twelve pounds. But the faces are rather faded and sometimes, in the crowd, they utter shocking screams, shrill as a screech-owl. . . .'

Beer and sherry appealed to the three young women Taine and his friend picked up in one of the secluded arbours. 'They drank moderately,' he reported. 'Our bookish English and their racy speech collided in a grotesque manner. One of them was very gay and wild: I have never seen such overflowing animal spirits. Another modest and quite pretty, rather subdued, was a milliner by trade, entirely dependent on herself. She has a friend who spends his Sundays with her. I looked at her carefully; it was clear she had the makings of an amiable and respectable girl. What had been the turning point?' Taine did not discover the answer to his question. He escorted the girls to the gate and paid their cab fares home without accompanying them. And on the whole he thought there was 'nothing brilliant, bold and smart' as in Paris about the spectacle of debauchery in London, whether at Cremorne or at the Argyle Rooms and the night dives around the Haymarket—it was merely rather depressing.

The shocking screams and the rowdy behaviour at Cremorne eventually brought strong complaints from the residents of Chelsea, who succeeded in getting the Pleasure Gardens suppressed in 1877. Greenwich Fair had also come to an end a few years earlier and bank holiday entertainment had moved to Hampstead Heath where the steam-driven roundabouts offered a new and more gaudy attraction to the public. Here, on the leafy hillside sloping away to the Vale of Health, the hurdy-gurdies, the swing-boats, the switchbacks and the merry-go-rounds whirled about in a glorious, giddy confusion and all the fun of the fair was enjoyed with a noisy gusto that set sobriety aside. There were streamers and rattles and paper hats; booths for everything—for the hairy woman and the elephant man, gypsy fortunes-tellers, ventriloquists and Bluebeard; shooting-galleries, peep-shows, and coconut shies; Sarsaparilla wine, monkey-nuts and

Queen Victoria and Prince Albert in Scotland
by Sir Edwin Landseer, RA, 1852

A Trip to Greenwich on Easter Monday, 1847

EASTER MONDAY ON THE RIVER THAMES.—GOING TO GREENWICH. 1847

Archery Meeting at the Crystal Palace, 1859

Tennis by George Du Maurier, 1880

A Musical Party in the Eighties by Fred Barnard

A 'Lion Comique' at the Oxford Music-hall in the Nineties by T. Pennell

The Great Exhibition, 1851. The Crystal Palace, Hyde Park

The Zoological Gardens in the Sixties

ice-cream. The cockney carts and the gypsy caravans, the
donkeys and the dogs and the children screaming all
added to the riotous, rip-roaring fun, which kept the more
sober-minded folk at home or sent them indoors to the
more edifying entertainment advertised at the Egyptian
Hall. There, on Whit Monday, they could enjoy 'Marvels
of instantaneous invisibility, Darwinism demented, flying
Heads, singing Flowers, marvellous transmutations of
plants and animals into Human Beings and startling trans-
formations in Fairy Land'—all for 1*s* in the area or 5*s*
for 'a sofa stall numbered and reserved'.

The Egyptian Hall entertainments and Tussaud's Wax-
works in Baker Street were designed for the family and
were perfectly innocuous; the museums of art and science
and natural history founded on the profits from the Great
Exhibition, and the concerts at the Crystal Palace, which
had been re-erected at Sydenham, catered for those who
combined their pleasure with a desire for self-improve-
ment. But the most popular entertainment in London
and the provinces was quite another matter, for in the
midst of Victorian prudery and priggishness the Music
Halls burst into song like a loud woman in a raffish hat
at a vicarage tea party. By the 1870s there were 347 of
them in London alone, ranging from the smallest, grub-
biest 'free-and-easies' in the tavern saloons of Hoxton
and Whitechapel to the red plush and glitter of the Oxford
and the Canterbury; and they offered a whole world of
uninhibited entertainment which was drawn from the
natural comic genius of the people and brewed up into
a marvellous, ribald concoction of winkles and champagne, toffs and swells, giddy girls and pint-sized cockney
comics.

From the very beginning this entertainment had been
an English phenomenon owing nothing to any outside
influence. Thackeray in the early years of the century had
known the shady taverns round about the Strand and

Covent Garden and their underground 'caves of har-
mony', where the bucks and the Bohemian *literati* met
at night to carouse with the lowest company and where
Edmund Kean had drunk himself into 'a drooping, pant-
ing and exhausted man'. And it was here, at the notorious
Cyder Cellars in Maiden Lane, that one of the first of the
professional entertainers, G. W. Ross, roused his audience
to a frenzy with his macabre and melodramatic song of
Sam Hall, the Chimney Sweep. Then, in the 1840s, a chorister
from the Royal Opera House, W. C. Evans, seeing the
possibilities of providing similar entertainment in less
sordid surroundings, converted what had been a nobleman's residence in Covent Garden into an hotel, turning
the handsome pillared dining-hall into a splendid song
and supper room with a platform stage. As many as eight
hundred people could be seated at the tables and served
with drinks from ten at night until two in the morning,
while they listened to the performers and joined in the
rollicking choruses. Ladies were excluded, though privileged members of the audience were occasionally
allowed to entertain a woman friend or two in the discreetly hidden little box at the side of the auditorium;
and the chairman, resplendent with a buttonhole and a
big cigar, kept order, sitting by the platform to introduce
each new performer with a rap of his hammer on the
table. It might be Sam Cowell singing *The Rat-Catcher's
Daughter* or *Villikins and his Dinah* for a guinea a week and
his supper each night, or Charles Sloman croaking his
ballad *The Maid of Judah*: a lot of smut was enjoyed and
a lot of drink and tobacco in the frowsty, smoky atmosphere of masculine good-fellowship and fun.

   But the most rapid development of the music halls
came in the next decade under the direction of Charles
Morton, an ex-pub-keeper from Hackney, who from
1850 until his death in 1904 at the age of eighty-five, was
the leading impresario of the lighter stage. His very first

venture was a success, when he took over the old Canterbury Arms on the Surrey side of the river and built a
magnificent hall there to hold fifteen hundred people.
By charging 6d for a seat at one of the tables and 9d in
the gallery, he was able to offer his patrons better entertainment than they had ever been accustomed to, and as
a talent spotter he never made a mistake. He discovered
George Leybourne, a mechanic from the Midlands whose
real name was Joe Saunders, performing in a sleazy
tavern in Whitechapel and promptly brought him to the
Canterbury, where his song *Champagne Charlie* created a
furore, and his dundreary whiskers, top hat and spats,
denoting the swell or the gent on the spree, set the
pattern for all the *lions comiques* of the day. He was soon
billed as the Great Leybourne to compete with his most
serious rival, the Great Vance, and was soon making a
fortune for himself which he spent like water, and a
fortune for Morton, who, more wisely, crossed the river
to conquer the West End with his new and still more
splendid hall, the Oxford.

Men could bring their wives or their women to these
new music halls, and the chairman at the Canterbury,
John Caulfield, introduced his own wife there in 1854 as
the first of the feminine serio-comic vocalists to appear
before a paying audience. Mrs Caulfield was not a very
talented artiste, but she led the way for those who were:
for Jenny Hill, 'the Vital Spark', for the two Bessies,
Bellwood and Bonehill, for Katie Lawrence and Nellie
Power, and that incomparable Queen of the Halls in the
nineties, Marie Lloyd. Nothing quite like the serio-
comics had ever been seen before—and nothing quite
like them was ever to be seen again, with their feathered
hats and frilly dresses, their racy gusto and their vulgarity,
their saucy smiles, nods and winks and wicked innuen-
does. It was not what they sang—it was how they did it,
with the sharp-edged, cynical humour of the streets and

the gas-light, instinctively mocking all that was smug and conventional in the Victorian code of respectability and deliberately turning it inside out.

Jenny Hill was the child of a cockney cab driver. Her career began in the rowdy East End taverns, where she scrubbed the floors in the morning and stood on a table at night to sing to the customers downing their porter. Married to an acrobat in her teens, she was stranded with a baby and not a penny in her pocket, when the manager of the London Pavilion took her on out of pity in 1869. She went on to the platform and sang:

> He's out on the fuddle, with a lot of his pals,
> Out on the fuddle, along with other gals;
>   He's always on the fuddle.
>   While I'm in such a muddle,
>   But I mean to have a legal separ-a-a-tion!

She was funny, she was sad; she had vitality and genius. And before long she was earning enough money to buy herself a large house at Streatham called The Hermitage, though anything less like a hermit's than her own gregarious way of life could never have been imagined. She entertained her friends with a reckless generosity common to all the music-hall artists when they were in funds and never said no to anyone in need. Guests arriving at ten o'clock on a Sunday morning were welcomed by the sound of champagne corks popping and were expected to stay for luncheon, tea in the garden and dinner late in the evening; and it was Jenny's footman, not Jenny herself, who was shocked when her greatest friend on the halls, Bessie Bellwood, brought a tray of winkles for tea and demanded a packet of pins to tackle them with.

Bessie, like Jenny, had known poverty, starting life as a rabbit-skinner in the New Cut and gravitating like a moth towards the bright lights of the halls. Neither of them had any leisure, and both burnt themselves out around the age of forty. But they lit up the often drab and sober struggle for existence of the men and women in their audience, and in their own lives enjoyed an absolute freedom from the prohibitions, the snobbery and the humbug of Victorian middle-class gentility. Bessie was boisterous and good-hearted and her riotous song *Wot Cheer, Ria!*, which she performed in a wine-coloured frock reaching to the ground in tiers of frills from the waist and a hat with a red and white swansdown feather, sent the boys in the gallery into shrieks of laughter.

She was still at the height of her career when Sickert started going to the music halls as a very young man in the seventies and found his inspiration in them for a whole series of paintings. He admired her cockney wit and enjoyed her company, often driving her in a hansom cab from one hall to another and going home with her to Gower Street for an ambrosial dish of tripe and onions and a pint of porter, before walking back to Hampstead in the small hours of the morning. She was at her best and most brilliant, he thought, when she performed in the smaller halls at Hoxton, Camden Town and Islington, where the atmosphere between the stage and the audience was more intimate than in the West End and she was encouraged to throw all decorum to the winds. Here the local lads of the district, the bowler-hatted clerks and warehousemen and the small shop-keepers came to forget their troubles in the warmth of the garish lights and the convivial vulgarity of an entertainment they understood. They came to laugh until their sides ached, to shout at the performers and pelt them with rotten eggs if they were displeased, to whistle and scream with delight—for to them the music hall was a feast of fun and a magic world, not a sophisticated taste in diversion.

But in the West End the halls were getting bigger and more luxurious. The handsome new London Pavilion

built in 1885, the Tivoli in the Strand, the new Alhambra
on one side of Leicester Square and the Empire on the
other were designed to appeal to the man-about-town in
search of pleasure. And at the same time the dingy
chop-houses, eating places and night dives around Piccadilly were being transformed into smart restaurants
where, in contrast to the dull and stuffy atmosphere in
the clubs, it was pleasant to dine and wine before going
out on the town. Max Beerbohm remembered being
'filled with an awful, but pleasant, sense of audacity' when
as a young undergraduate, he dined at the Café Royal for
the first time and went on to the London Pavilion. He
was, he declared, 'relieved, though slightly disappointed
also, at finding that the Pavilion seemed very like a
theatre, except that the men around us were mostly
smoking and not in evening clothes, and that there was
alongside of the stalls an extensive drinking-bar, of which
the barmaids were the only—or almost the only—ladies
present, and that the stage was occupied by one man
only.' This was none other than the Great Macdermott,
the *lion comique* who had set the town on fire in 1878 with
his rousing ditty *We Don't Want to fight, but by Jingo, if We
Do!* 'Here he was, in the flesh, in the greasepaint, surviving and thriving. . . . a huge old burly fellow with a
yellow wig and a vast expanse of crumpled shirt front
that had in the middle of it, a very large, not *very* real
diamond stud.' And he was followed by 'a very elastic
and electric little creature with twists and turns of face
and body and voice as many as the innumerable pearl
buttons that adorned his jacket and his breeches'—
Albert Chevalier, who had only just made his debut as
a coster comedian with his *Knocked 'em in the Old Kent
Road* and his celebrated song *My Old Dutch*.

This was the heyday of the music halls with Dan Leno,
Little Tich, Vesta Tilley and Marie Lloyd topping the
bill after her giddy climb up the ladder from the Grecian

Saloon in the City Road via Hoxton, Bermondsey and the Old Mo' in Drury Lane. All were stars of the first magnitude, rich in talent and generous in giving. They had technique, guts and gaiety; individuality and genius. They worked hard and long at their apparently frivolous pursuit of amusing the public and, more often than not, died in harness. But their songs were famous all round the world and they held their own with superb confidence when stage spectacles and ballet were introduced into the music-hall programmes to satisfy a more luxurious taste in entertainment.

At the Empire the new taste was catered for on the most lavish scale and the promenade at the back of the royal circle, with its shaded lights and voluptuous velvet-covered couches, became the most notorious rendezvous in London for the fashionable man-about-town and the *demi-mondaine*. The swish of a silk skirt and the nodding invitation of the parma violets tucked lightly into an ample corsage were a prelude to the evening and the private hansom cab waiting outside in the square. And although the promenade was heavily attacked as a hotbed of vice by the indignant reformer Mrs Ormiston Chant, neither she nor her associates, who were nicknamed 'prudes on the prowl', could restrain the frou-frou and the fun. A more extravagant attitude towards leisure and pleasure had already infected the gas-lit London of the eighties and in the next decade was to stir up and remove part of the huge mountain of Victorian respectability.

13

FIN DE SIÈCLE

THE REBELLION BEGAN in the Aesthetic Movement, which grew out of two distinct branches of artistic aspiration: the Pre-Raphaelite Brotherhood, started in the 1850s by Dante Gabriel Rossetti, Millais and Holman Hunt, and the new Bohemianism brought into England in the sixties by a small man in a large straw hat and a white duck suit, with dark, observant eyes, black curly hair with a curious white streak in it and an air of immaculate epicureanism. There was nothing much in common between this uncommon man whose name was James McNeill Whistler and the artists of the Brotherhood; yet for a time one reflected on the other and combined to undermine the generally accepted standards of taste in Victorian London, where those who concerned themselves with art required a picture to tell a story.

The Pre-Raphaelites, supported by Ruskin, were inspired by a high moral purpose. Their aim was serious— to redeem painting from its academic insincerity and to return to a happier epoch than their own competitive age of industrial expansion by re-invoking the mystical, romantic medievalism of the past. Millais deserted the Brotherhood soon after his marriage to Effie Ruskin and became a much honoured academician; Hunt went abroad and occupied himself with religion. But William Morris and Edward Burne-Jones, as ardent young disciples of Rossetti, formed a new triumvirate after the original one had broken up. Morris, with his wallpapers, pottery, hand-woven fabrics and uncomfortable oak furniture, preached the gospel of beauty in the home undefiled by commercial exploitation, in the belief that this would pave the way for a Utopian improvement of life for everyone. Burne-Jones retreated successfully into a world of Arthurian legend, where knights loitered palely in the woods and sad damsels awaited their coming among the sinuous fronds of a symbolic creeper or the ivy-clad ruins of a moated grange—so successfully that he was himself knighted by a grateful Queen Victoria in 1894. But Rossetti—by far the most imaginative and talented member of the Brotherhood, ever striving to realize the exotic emotionalism of his Latin temperament in highly coloured poetry and paint—came to a tragic end as a neurotic drug addict.

After the death of his wife, Elizabeth Siddal, from an overdose of laudanum, and his somewhat theatrical gesture of laying his poems between her hair and her cheek before her burial in remorse for his neglect of her, he had retired to a large house in Chelsea, where he was able to indulge his enthusiasm for collecting curious animals, bric-à-brac and china. A zebu, proving to be altogether too excitable in captivity, had to be sent away; but a wombat, described by him as 'a joy, a triumph, a delight and a madness', slept over the dining-table, and a kangaroo hopped in the garden. Brass pots, dulcimers, antique chests filled with old costumes, jewellery and strangely wrought candlesticks littered his studio, and

his four-poster bed was hung with thick curtains embroidered with fruit and flowers. Everything around him
was quaint and old and in a fearful clutter of Bohemian
disorder and dust.

This queer taste—or lack of taste—did not appeal
very much to Whistler when the two artists were introduced to each other by Swinburne, but it amused him.
Whistler's Bohemianism, learnt from the new men in
Paris, from Manet and Degas and the other artists who
frequented the Café Guerbois, was of quite a different
order; it belonged to Henri Murger's *La Vie de Bohème*
and to the clarion call to the new generation devised by
Theophile Gautier and Charles Baudelaire, *L'art pour
l'Art*, soon to be translated into English as Art for Art's
Sake. The Latin Quarter in Paris had, in fact, no correspondence whatever with the stained glass, Gothic mood
of resuscitation practised by Rossetti and his disciples;
the Frenchmen looked forward to new forms of expression, the Englishmen backward to a never-never land of
their romantic dreams. Yet it was Whistler who introduced to the Pre-Raphaelites the new Parisian craze for
collecting Japanese prints, blue and white porcelain, fans
and screens and ginger jars—a cult that spread quickly
into the drawing-rooms of Kensington and Belgravia,
bringing the gospel of aestheticism to the ladies of leisure
who wished to be thought 'interesting'.

Simultaneously the *Poems and Ballads* of Swinburne,
published in 1866, which horrified the more conven-
tionally minded bourgeoisie by their torrential freedom
of expression, and the mysterious, mystical teaching of
Walter Pater at Oxford, suggested the alluring prospect
of 'new passion for daytime and night' and a new,
romantic approach to the forbidden pleasures of sin. To
be modern was to be intense, to dress peculiarly—the
ladies in flowing draperies and beads and the gentlemen
in velvet jackets; to collect blue and white china, to yearn

after culture and to mix devotion to art with a daring liberty from the restrictions of middle-class morality. The more *Punch* criticized and mocked at the new woman, the more intense she became in her brooding solitude, modelled on the attitudes of the late Elizabeth Siddal and the living Jane Morris, and the more du Maurier joked about the loose collar and flowing tie of the aesthetic undergraduate with his passion for the lily and the sunflower, the more he advertised the increasing notoriety of Oscar Wilde.

'I do not seek happiness,' Wilde declared, 'but Pleasure which is more tragic'—a prophetic utterance that his conquest of London in the late seventies appeared for the moment to belie. For as soon as this brilliant young Irishman came down from Oxford as a self-styled Professor of Aesthetics with the ideas of Pater buzzing in his head, he created a furore at Whistler's Sunday breakfast parties in Tite Street. Whistler's famous libel action against Ruskin was still the talk of the town. His spirited defence of the doctrine of Art for Art's Sake, his devastating wit and his arrogance, no less than the haunting poetry to be found in his paintings and etchings of Chelsea, had given him a commanding position as the master of the aesthetic world, and Wilde at once became his disciple. But it was not a relationship that could bear the strain of two such egotistical temperaments for very long and soon it was Oscar, not Whistler, who was the talk of the town, and Bunthorne, in Gilbert and Sullivan's opera *Patience*, who stole the limelight and set the fashion for the serio-comic pose of the arty young man at war with the Philistines.

Wilde was good at advertising himself and quite incapable of playing second fiddle to anyone else. He blandly ignored the growing enmity of Whistler and made a staggering success of his lecture tour in America. Then he went to Paris and swapped the aesthetic pose for the gay, cosmopolitan *flaneur*, sipping absinthe and smoking scented cigarettes; and he found in the decadent writers Baudelaire, Verlaine, Rimbaud and Huysmans, a *beauté maudite* that was infinitely more alluring than anything he had learnt from Walter Pater, 'a pleasure that was poisonous, all shimmering in purple and gold', only to be achieved through voluptuous experiment, exhaustion and excess. Back in London, he cultivated an epigrammatic style of conversation, polishing his elegant Irish wit into a rapier of steel and, with a dazzling thrust in the air, cutting to pieces the accepted principles of even the most advanced members of the intelligentsia. He was deliberately 'shocking', deliberately 'wicked', and all with a gaiety and a fascination that people found enthralling—or insufferable. 'Nothing succeeds like ex-

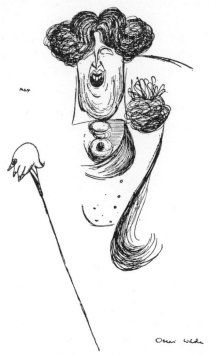

Oscar Wilde, by Max Beerbohm

cess,' he declared; and at the Café Royal with its glittering mirrors reflecting the Parisian style décor of gilt caryatids, marble-topped tables and red plush, he held court among his friends and his enemies, indulging in 'that inordinate passion for pleasure, which is the secret of remaining young.'

Pleasure and still more pleasure was the cry of the Café Royal society, riding high on the *fin de siècle* tide of ennui, extravagance and artificiality. Here came Ernest Dowson, 'desolate and sick of an old passion', crying for 'madder music, stronger wine'; George Moore with his moon-white face and fishy eyes, looking for a substitute for the stimulating café society of Paris; Frank Harris with his flashy, tall stories, fabricated for his own amusement to exhibit his capacity as a Don Juan; Arthur Symons boasting that 'a good poem about the scent in a sachet' had as much aesthetic value as 'a good poem about a flower in the hedge'; Richard Le Gallienne, Max Beerbohm, Sickert, Charles Conder and Aubrey Beardsley, a frail and consumptive clerk in the Guardian Insurance Office, who suddenly took London by storm with his black and white drawings.

The art of Beardsley—decadent, elaborate and suggestive of a secret inner world of sexual aberration—expressed the whole spirit of the nineties. He invented, or revealed from within his own frenetic nature, a fantastic, Stygian universe of perverse, epicene figures in a grotesque landscape, where the very flowers of the field had a corrupt elegance and artificiality. The serpentine arrogance and depraved beauty of his line conveyed a shocking familiarity with the evils of self-indulgence, ennui and erotic experience. Working at night by candlelight with the hectic impetuosity of one who knew he was doomed to die young, he was obsessed by a craving to shine among the great, and succeeded brilliantly, his fame passing beyond the small coterie of the initiated to

reach a wider audience after the appearance of the first
number of the *Yellow Book* in 1894.

Beardsley posters appeared on the hoardings and the
Beardsley woman became the rage. Popular newspapers
and magazines took him up to praise or condemn his
extraordinary talent. *Punch* printed an amusing parody
on Tennyson's *Lady Clara Vere de Vere*, which began:

> Mr Aubrey Beer de Beers
>   You're getting quite a high renown;
> Your comedy of Leers, you know,
>   Is posted all about the town.

Yet this sudden onrush of notoriety did not turn Beardsley's head. He enjoyed the fuss with a restless, light-
hearted gaiety that covered over his sickness and his
suffering. Bright lights, people, parties and the music
halls appealed to his desire for excitement and stimulated
his curiosity without interfering with his compulsive
attitude to his work. 'When I first met him,' Max Beerbohm wrote, 'I thought I had never seen so utterly frail
a creature—he looked more like a ghost than a living
man. When I came to know him better, I realized that it
was only by sheer force of nerves that he contrived to
sustain himself. He was always, whenever one saw him,
in the highest spirits, full of fun and of fresh theories
about life and art. But one could not help feeling that as
soon as he was alone he would sink down, fatigued and
listless, with all the spirit gone out of him.'

Beerbohm's comment was exact, and the witty carica-
tures he drew of Beardsley distilled the very essence of
the young man's character. Max, indeed, as an acute
observer of his contemporaries, seldom made an error
of judgement. He practised the art of being a spectator
of the nineties and enjoyed a very private pleasure in
watching and listening and recording his impressions by

the stroke of a pen more deadly than a pin. 'A delicate and Tory temperament precludes me from conversing with the Radicals,' he declared, and it was precisely his delicacy, his urbanity and his superbly civilized approach to life that set him apart from his fellow men. His manners were exquisite. He talked quietly, dressed with consummate elegance and adopted a pose of elderly, unruffled calm, all the more fascinating in a young man of four and twenty; and while he laughed gently at the folly of his friends, he was equally quick to smile at his own foibles. Anything bombastic, pretentious, vain or self-deceiving was the target for his fastidious, ironic humour, his prominent blue eyes probing meticulously under the skin like the tip of a surgeon's scalpel. And he had no desire to climb higher in society or to become involved with the essential vulgarity of the *fin de siècle*; he was content with his pleasure in the art of living gracefully on the fringe of a highly experimental era.

Oscar Wilde, meanwhile, was adding glamour to his reputation as a wit by his writings. *The Picture of Dorian Gray*, published in 1891, was more than a *succès d'estime*. None of his later works, he declared, gave him so much pleasure to write, none proved so daringly that the philosophy of Art for Art's Sake, if pursued to its ultimate end, could only be satisfied by exploring the sensational depths of 'the sin without a name'. Homosexuality was not expressed, but implied; and was not stated, but insinuated even more explicitly in Wilde's *Intentions* published the same year, in which he remarked: 'There is something tragic about the enormous number of young men there are in England at the present moment who start life with perfect profiles, and end by adopting some useful profession.' Not that this was true of his new acquaintance Lord Alfred Douglas, the son of Lord Queensberry, 'the scarlet Marquis'—'Bosie' had no intention of adopting any profession useful or otherwise, except that of a playboy and the spoilt darling of his infatuated friend.

Wilde was married with two children and at the height of his career. His plays, combining style and stylishness in a manner that had not been seen since the Restoration, outclassed the work of all the other dramatists then writing for the theatre with the possible exception of Pinero. His characters—Lord Darlington, Lord Illingworth and Lord Goring—boasted of their idleness, their egotism and their pleasure in being wicked, in the epigrammatic dialogue of high comedy. Oscar, the tightrope walker in life, was a supreme juggler with words on the stage. And the first night of *The Importance of Being Earnest*, put on at the St James's Theatre by George Alexander, was a glittering social event. All London was there, in spite of a bitter wind and deep snow: *not* to be seen at this gala was to be a social outcast. But one gentleman, who arrived with a bag of rotten vegetables, was refused admittance—'the scarlet Marquis' had talked too much about his intention to flay the dramatist in public and was kept out by the police.

'One should be careful to choose one's enemies well' was another of Oscar's epigrams—only this time he had misjudged his man, and instead of ignoring Queensberry's rude note left at the Albemarle Club twenty-four hours later, he brought a libel action against him. No doubt Wilde had Whistler's celebrated case against Ruskin in mind and, egged on by Lord Alfred Douglas, believed he could show the world once and for all that artists were immune from the laws of the Philistines; but again he had misjudged the occasion and the temper of the court where the case was heard. The Old Bailey was not the Café Royal; the solemn men on the jury were not carried away by the notion that a love letter to a young man, to 'those red-leaf lips of yours . . . made . . . for the madness of kissing', was a prose poem; and, as the evidence mounted against Wilde, gradually revealing a sordid tangle of unnatural vice behind the scenes of his brilliant career, it became obvious to his friends that nothing could save him from a worse ordeal except flight across the Channel. Some remnant of arrogance, perhaps an inverted kind of heroism, for he was never wanting in courage, induced him to stay and defy his inquisitors. He was arrested and committed for trial on a criminal charge and when the jury disagreed, tried a second time and sentenced to the maximum term of two years' imprisonment, which the judge, Mr Justice Wills, believed was 'totally inadequate' for a crime that he considered was 'more horrible than murder'.

The case roused the triumphant Philistines to an orgy of self-righteous indignation. The Press poured out a dark stream of vituperation that excited the instinct for sensation in the public mind. Pamphlets were hawked in the streets, reproducing the meatier bits of the case and giving much satisfaction to the prurience lurking behind the respectable frock-coat and waistcoat of many a Victorian husband and father. Those who disliked art because they could not understand it, and those who frowned on pleasure took a fierce, pagan delight in the sacrifice of their victim and enjoyed themselves immensely in the process. Wilde's name was expunged from the playbills of *The Importance of Being Earnest*, his books withdrawn from circulation, his house and all his goods sold off to meet the cost of bankruptcy. The whole gaudy bubble of his reputation was pricked like an air balloon and lay limp on the ground. Yet his tragic addiction to pleasure had made its mark. Gas-lit London, with Lottie Collins singing *Ta-ra-ra-boom-deay* at the top of her voice, suppressed his name and shuddered at the awfulness of his crime, but did not lose its raffish gaiety or the new freedom of enjoyment Wilde had done so much to encourage.

Lights blazed at the Empire and the Alhambra, at the Café Royal, Kettner's, and Romano's in the Strand. Hansom cabs jingled in the streets and the man-about-town in his opera-cloak and opera-hat, with his white gloves and his big cigar, was awake until the morning. The nineteenth century had come full circle. Wit or money, as in the days of the Regency, could buy almost anything: licence and liberty, leisure and pleasure, the entreé into high society, debauchery or vice. But the self-indulgence of the nineties was of a different kind from the Regency whirl—less full-blooded, more sophisticated, more decadent, not so young. The new voluptuaries were tired men and more self-conscious, deliberately flouting the rules of conduct practised by the more sober half of the nation, which had scarcely existed in the time of the Regent. The views on morality of the middle classes had more substance now, more power and more influence; they could not be so easily ignored.

At the top of society, the Prince of Wales and the fast, cosmopolitan set revolving round him at Marlborough House, had not escaped criticism. It shocked Mr Gladstone and public opinion when the heir to the throne was involved in the Mordaunt divorce case in 1870, admitting in his evidence that he was in the habit of taking a hansom cab when he wished to visit a friend *incognito*. Some years later the Tranby Croft case of cheating at cards created a worse scandal; it proved only too well that the Prince was a man of pleasure and not over-sensitive about the company he kept. It was one thing to enjoy racing, shooting and yachting, trips to Paris and Bad Homburg, nights at the opera and even at the music halls, but another thing altogether to forfeit the respect of the nation by gambling at cards. No one knew quite what went on at the opulent house parties in the country—that was rumour; the discovery that His Royal Highness actually travelled about with his own set of crested counters to lay on the green baize tables at baccarat was a serious revelation of fact.

And there were the fashionable, beautiful women who were not always discreet. The well-bred among them remained silent and shrank from too much publicity; but that dazzling, cold creature from the Isle of Jersey, Lily Langtry, who swept through the London drawing-rooms in the seventies with Mr Langtry following meekly behind her, had only to appear in the Park driving in her open carriage for everyone to climb on to the chairs in a wild attempt to catch a glimpse of her. It was common knowledge that the Prince would go nowhere unless Mrs Langtry had also been invited; and when her dizzy round of one London season after another had emptied Mr Langtry's purse to the bottom, it was the Prince of Wales who used his influence to put her on the stage. She was thus able to begin at the top of the profession with no acting experience and to insist that a red carpet should be rolled out from her dressing-room into the wings of the Princess's Theatre, where she played her own version of Shakespeare's serpent of old Nile in *Antony and Cleopatra*. The fabulous cost of her clothes and her jewellery was well advertised in advance and she lay invitingly on a leopard skin couch, but the money she spent on the production was not her own, so it did not matter very much that the public took little pleasure in her performance after the first excitement had worn off.

Theatre-going had changed remarkably since the days when Queen Victoria and Prince Albert had seen fit to encourage Mr and Mrs Charles Kean in their efforts to elevate the drama from the low state it had fallen into. With the music halls drawing away the more boisterous elements of the public, polite society was enticed back into the auditorium by the Bancrofts, who developed a new style of naturalistic acting in the 'cup and saucer' plays written for them by Tom Robertson. They took immense care with their productions, appealing directly to the intelligence of their audience; and they also reduced the bill to a single piece, with perhaps a curtain raiser, cutting out the more debased forms of entertainment which for so long had satisfied the depraved taste of the *hoi polloi*, and thus inaugurating a new era of respectability in the theatre.

At the Lyceum, Henry Irving and Ellen Terry put new life into Shakespeare and into the romantic melodramas that suited Irving's style of acting so well, their magnetism drawing an ever widening circle of admirers, and Irving's dignity as a man earning for the theatrical profession its first respectable honour when he was knighted in 1895. At the same time the Gilbert and Sullivan operas launched by D'Oyly Carte at the Savoy Theatre, established a new standard of musical entertainment wherein the sly humour and sentiment of Gilbert's lyrics combined with Sullivan's fund of melody could offend no one and entertain everyone. The patronage of fashionable society ensured their success; and it was the white ties and the diamonds in the orchestra stalls that lent a similar distinction to the St James's Theatre, where George Alexander's good looks and gentlemanly manner, quite apart from his acting ability, gave prestige to the society drama of Wilde and Pinero. The more humble patrons up in the gallery or down in the pit were thrilled by the scenes of High Life being enacted before their eyes—on the stage and in the auditorium; and when Mrs Patrick Campbell appeared as Paula in *The Second Mrs Tanqueray* in 1893, the daring of her performance created a sensation.

But the new freedom of thought that characterized the nineties was not to be found in the established repertory of Irving at the Lyceum or in the society drama of Pinero at the St James's. Ibsen's *Ghosts* was put on by the Independent Theatre of J. T. Grein in 1891 and damned by Clement Scott as 'an open drain, a dirty act done publicly and a lazaar house with all its doors and windows open'. Anyone who enjoyed such 'filth' was not a fit member of society. Yet to George Bernard Shaw Ibsen's drama was a revelation and a challenge. What the Norwegian could do, the Irishman could surely do better. If the great actor managers would not look at his plays and the Lord Chamberlain would not license them, he would still continue to write them and to publish them, which he did in 1898 as *Plays: Pleasant and Unpleasant*.

The audacity and the originality of his opinions, his Irish capacity for turning somersaults in public and tilting at the ostrich-like complacency of society in general, satisfied his own vanity and intrigued his progressive, intellectual friends in the Fabian Society. He was a blue-eyed, red-bearded jaeger giant among them: irresponsible and fascinating, sometimes repellent, but always stimulating. Having no truck with the decadent theory of Art for Art's Sake, he none the less maintained that art was 'the subtlest, the most seductive, the most effective means of propagandism in the world', and both as a critic and as a dramatist, he set out to prove it. He was furious with Irving for his indifference towards the revolutionary work of Ibsen and worried Ellen Terry like a dog, until she eventually lost confidence in herself and in Irving when both of them were too old to change. Yet she defended her position with courage and common sense. 'I never said *Borkman* was a "poor" play. What do you mean?' she wrote in one of her letters to Shaw. 'I say the effect on an audience would be to depress, to make unhappy, to make less hopeful some of us who long to dream a little. I think the theatre should gladden tired working people. I cannot imagine a greater happiness coming to me than to be well enough and free enough to just act "for nothing" all round England in little dull narrow-minded poky places. . . . But do you think I'd

give them *Borkman*? Poor dear people. No. They should
have *The Tempest* with such lovely enchanting fairies,
such graceful young things, such a lot of warm yellow
limelight sunshine. They should have *Much Ado, The
Merchant of Venice, Merry Wives* . . . oh, and heaps of
crowds and nice things. . . . It's all very shocking this, I
believe you will tell me, but for why, I can't think.'

He did tell her it was shocking. He told her it was
sentimental and absurd, but she remained tender and
loving and unrepentant. And it was no use arguing—the
romantic escapism of the Lyceum just did not mix with
the bare realism of the new drama, any more than Ellen's
pleasure in the irresistible love letters Shaw was writing
to her almost every other day would have survived if
they had attempted to make their fantasy real. And he
was soon telling her about his 'green-eyed Irish millionairess, Miss P–T, who has had cleverness and character
enough to decline that station of life—"great catch for
somebody"—to which it pleased God to call her,' adding
impishly: 'I am going to refresh my heart by falling in
love with her, but mind—only with her, not with the
million, so someone else must marry her, if she can stand
him after me.' Ellen was naturally curious to meet her,
but Shaw refused. 'You'd feel instantly with her that the
dressing-room was the *wrong* scene for the *right* line,' he
wrote cryptically and Ellen had to content herself with
peeping at them both through the curtain between the
acts of *Cymbeline*.

Shaw was exaggerating as usual. Charlotte Payne-
Townsend was not a millionairess, though she was very
well off and in many ways typical of the 'new' woman—
the intelligent woman who could no longer tolerate the
restrictions of a life of useless leisure bounded by social
trivialities and domesticity. 'Bred up in a second-rate
fashionable society without any education or habit of
work, she found herself at about thirty-three years of age

alone in the world, without ties, without any definite
creed and with a large income'—thus Beatrice Webb
described her soon after their first meeting. 'For the last
four years she has drifted about—in India, in Italy, in
Egypt, in London, seeking occupation and fellow spirits.
In person she is attractive—a large graceful woman with
masses of chocolate brown hair, pleasant grey eyes, matte
complexion which sometimes looks muddy, at other
times forms a picturesquely pale background to her
brilliant hair and bright eyes. . . . She dresses well—in
her flowing white evening robe she approaches beauty.
At moments she is plain. By temperament she is an
anarchist—feeling any regulation or rule intolerable—
a tendency which has been exaggerated by her irresponsible wealth. She is a romantic, but thinks herself
cynical. She is a socialist and a radical, not because she
understands the Collectivist standpoint, but because she
is by nature a rebel . . . sympathetic and genuinely anxious
to increase the world's enjoyment and diminish the
world's pain.'

Whether or not this close analysis of her character
would have pleased Miss Payne-Townsend as much as
it obviously pleased Mrs Sidney Webb in making it, is
questionable. Beatrice Webb was now set in her ways
and an ardent social reformer, with an alarming capacity
for doing good to others in the way she believed good
should be done. The 'Collectivist standpoint' was a holy
crusade which she pursued with the narrow-minded
egotism and the zeal of a Victorian Joan of Arc. She
promptly persuaded her new friend to subscribe £1,000
towards the library of the New School of Economics
founded by the Fabian Society; she could never resist
a contribution towards the funds of the Society or the
opportunity of indoctrinating others with her own and
Sidney's opinions. Yet for Charlotte Payne-Townsend
the discovery of socialism and above all the chance it

gave her of coming into contact with people who believed so passionately in unconventional, new ideas, was exhilarating. It seemed at last that she had found a faith in life to offset her feeling of loneliness and frustration; and her first holiday with the Webbs and Bernard Shaw, when they roamed the countryside on their bicycles and Shaw, the philanderer, set out to dazzle her, gave her intense pleasure.

They laughed and quarrelled and talked all night long, and fell off their bicycles going too fast round a corner. Mrs Webb was 'interested, though a little uneasy' when she saw what was happening; she doubted whether Shaw could be 'induced to marry' and whether Charlotte could be happy without it. 'These warm-hearted unmarried women of a certain age are audacious and almost childishly reckless of consequences,' she noted—rather smugly, from the safe harbour of her own partnership with Sidney. But Charlotte herself was quite willing to face the consequences when she did finally become Mrs George Bernard Shaw, and Mrs Webb was satisfied. For one thing it put Shaw in his place and made this maddening, disturbing Irishman less of a menace to her own virtue. Shaw's flippancies were dangerous. 'Sidney's achievements are worth all Shaw's brilliance,' she asserted more than once—perhaps to convince herself that in choosing to become the helpmate of her high-principled and pragmatical spouse, she had not been wrong.

14

THE NEW
FREEDOM

MRS SIDNEY WEBB and her Fabian friends were not the
only women to be inspired by the new ideas fermenting
in the last quarter of the century. From the easy-going
background of upper middle-class leisure a number of
other ladies of exceptional ability were emerging with
revolutionary views on the need for better education and
wider opportunities for their sex. No longer content
with the haphazard teaching of an indigent governess
based on Miss Magnell's *Historical and Miscellaneous
Questions* ranging from 'What is Whalebone?' to 'Are not
Umbrellas of great Antiquity?', they believed girls were
capable of responding to a more advanced form of
tuition and that a little drawing and painting and beadwork
were not enough to qualify them for the rest of their lives.

There was Miss Emily Davies, the daughter of an
Anglican clergyman, whose demure and gentle appearance and modest style of dress concealed the heart and
the mind of an indomitable fighter. After fortifying herself with claret and biscuits, she appeared in person
before the Schools' Inquiry Commission and forced the

gentlemen on the board to look into the deplorable condition of girls' schools throughout the country. Then she badgered the universities to open their examinations to women students and, having gathered half a dozen young ladies together in a house at Hitchin, persuaded some of the Cambridge dons to come and lecture to them—an experiment which proved to be so successful that she was soon able to lay the foundations of Girton College.

At the same time, Miss Anne Jemima Clough, a sister of the poet Arthur Hugh Clough, was invited by Henry Sidgwick to become the first Principal of Newnham College, founded in 1871. Miss Clough was less militant in her methods than Miss Davies and kind to her students, tactfully holding the balance between their enthusiasm and the decorum she believed was necessary in their conduct if they were to escape criticism. When Professor Sidgwick heard they were wearing 'tied-back' dresses, then very much in the fashion, she called her girls together and suggested that perhaps they could untie their skirts in the lecture room, though when Mary Paley and Mary Kennedy went off on their own to Ely for a day of pleasure, she issued a new rule that 'students wishing to make expeditions in the neighbourhood must ask permission from the Principal'. Mary Paley was twenty-three and Mary Kennedy twenty-six; neither was a flibbertigibbet—they were both serious young students with no wish to draw attention to themselves. But their still more daring escapade of going to London and spending the night there when Professor Sidgwick got married at St James's Church, Piccadilly, so shocked Mary Paley's clerical father that he sent her fourteen-year-old brother post haste after the two girls to act as their chaperon, expressing his extreme displeasure in no uncertain manner and not, as his daughter wrote afterwards, forgiving her for a very long time.

Masculine opposition to feminine independence was, indeed, implacable in some quarters. Oxford was even more reluctant than Cambridge in opening its gates to the ladies. Dr Pusey and his clerical colleagues were appalled at the thought of women learning to think for themselves; Dr Liddon believed it was 'an educational development which runs counter to the wisdom and experience of all the centuries of Christendom', and Ruskin refused 'to let the bonnets in' to his lectures on art at the Sheldonian Theatre. None of all this, however, could prevent some of the more progressive wives and sisters of the dons from putting their bonnets together; and in 1879, with the help of a committee called the Association for the Education of Women, two 'Academical Houses for Women' were founded. They were hastily furnished in the cheapest possible way and were very ugly, but to the students, seen through the rose-tinted spectacles of their miraculous escape from home into a new world of scholarship and freedom, they were heavenly mansions.

The first Principal of Somerville, Miss Madeleine Shaw Lefevre, was a charming, serene lady, who loved gardening and was a keen amateur artist. She remarked that she felt 'quite unsuited' to her new position, having enjoyed a life of upper-class leisure and pleasure mixed with a certain amount of philanthropic work until the age of forty-four. Yet her background and her breeding were precisely the qualities most needed to ensure the success of this daring innovation and to demonstrate its seriousness of purpose. Far from being unwomanly or fast, the students were content to copy the style of their Principal. They dressed demurely in trailing velveteen gowns with wide lace collars on their sloping shoulders, or—in imitation of Walter Pater's sister Clara—aesthetically, in peacock blue serge ornamented with crewel-stitched sunflowers and amber beads. They did not, as some of their masculine opponents hoped they would, collapse in fainting fits at their lectures or try to influence their tutors with the more obvious feminine wiles. Their behaviour was irreproachable—it could not really be otherwise, since they were chaperoned wherever they went; but the pride and the pleasure they took in being the pioneers of a new independence stayed with them all their lives.

With equally impeccable antecedents as the Principal of Somerville, Miss Elizabeth Wordsworth, being a great-niece of the poet and the eldest daughter of the Bishop of Lincoln, ran the affairs of Lady Margaret Hall for thirty years with courage and distinction. Details of administration did not concern her very much—she kept the College correspondence in a shoe-box; but she believed in diversion for her students and a healthy enjoyment of life, recommending cold baths and long walks in the meadows, as well as becoming an enthusiastic advocate of games. At the age of fifty, she took up cycling, without apparently being in the least incommoded by the long skirts and high collars she wore as befitted the daughter of a bishop and the Principal of an Oxford College, and her amazing vitality continued to inspire everyone around her until within a few months of her death at the age of ninety-two. She once said that 'Adam was a poor thing until he had Eve', though she had little sympathy with those who were beginning to talk of 'women's rights'. Theoretical argument made no appeal to her lively mind; all her wisdom was directed towards a sane and balanced outlook for the young women in her charge, who had broken away from the frustrated and aimless existence of the unmarried daughter at home to make their own future in the world.

And it was not only the intellectuals who were breaking away from the restrictions of Victorian home life with its mundane domesticity and countless prohibitions.

Women everywhere were becoming more athletic, less timid, more ambitious. In the country the well-to-do went hunting, riding to hounds with as much zest as their menfolk, while others escaped abroad and even dared to go mountain-climbing, their hats tied on with veils and their feminine feet in sensible boots. They no longer played up to being afraid—or if they were, they concealed their terror and sought pleasure in being adventurous.

At least one exceptional woman, Miss Alma Beaumont, saw no reason why if men could jump out of a balloon, she could not do the same, and having made up her mind, no one could dissuade her from attempting this perilous feat. She admitted afterwards that she was 'a trifle nervous' before her first jump in 1888; but in spite of being 'rendered almost insane by that most terrible of all horrors, the horror of the empty air' before her parachute opened like a big umbrella, she so enjoyed the next sensation of 'floating in mid-air as lightly as an india-rubber doll at the end of a piece of elastic', that she never missed an opportunity of trying it again. Once she landed in a limekiln and another time in the rear of an express train travelling to Manchester, without her pleasure or her enthusiasm being in the least diminished by such an uncomfortable return to earth. 'I don't think parachuting is any more dangerous than riding a spirited horse across a stiff bit of country with hounds in full cry,' she asserted, 'and I speak from experience, for I have tried both.'

Hunting undoubtedly stimulated an intrepid outlook— and men could admire a good horsewoman without losing their self-esteem. A brave woman was easier to get on with than a clever one, and a well-tailored riding-habit could be very attractive. A pretty woman driving a pony or a high stepping horse also had charm, but it was doubtful whether the new horseless carriages on view at the first International Exhibition of Motors held

at the Imperial Institute in London in 1896, would ever
be more than a mechanical toy to amuse the sterner sex.
Going for a drive as a passenger on one of these fractious
and noisy vehicles was adventurous enough, and it was
thought that the ladies could never be trusted to hold
the steering wheel in their dainty hands or to press down
the pedals with their delicate feet. Yet Mrs Bernard
Weguelin of Coombe End, near Malden, a lady of quite
extraordinary grace and charm, acquired a 3½ h.p. De
Dion in 1897 and after an hour or so driving in the
country lanes round Coombe Hill 'to get the hang of the
thing', drove herself all the way back to her town house
in Pont Street twenty miles off without any mishap and
without showing any sign of fatigue. The next year she
toured the country with her husband and 'to the utter
mystification of all lookers-on, to whom the spectacle
of a lady on a car was altogether new', was often to be
seen at the wheel 'negotiating down Bond Street and
Piccadilly'.

Less spirited ladies naturally looked on motoring as
an eccentric new sport for the rich and preferred milder
amusements. Bazaars, garden parties and flower shows,
gossip and tea parties, their ailments and their music
and visiting the poor, still occupied a great deal of their
time, and their leisure was still a privilege they owed to
the number of servants they employed. Ladies, in fact,
were still ladies; they did not do things for themselves,
they told other people what to do and how to do it. But
the young Victorian miss with her scrapbook and her
album, her dried flowers, her seaweed and her shells,
had put her crinoline aside, and though still encased in
'a cuirasse bodice' and encumbered by a bustle, had discovered a new freedom of movement. The amiable games
of croquet she had once enjoyed were out of date and
old-fashioned compared with the mania for tennis, which
swept like a wind of change through the quiet country-

side and brought the sexes together on the courts in a
wave of exciting activity. The gentlemen wore knickerbockers and long black stockings; the ladies tied their
long dresses back with an apron with pockets in it for
spare tennis balls and ran about with little straw hats
firmly pinned on to their hair, determined to show off
their athletic abilities.

'I am just learning and it is certainly livelier movement
than I have indulged in for many a day,' the American
wife of Richard Jebb wrote from Cambridge to her sister
in Philadelphia—and with the somewhat dictatorial tone
she often used towards her nieces: 'The girls *ought* to
play lawn tennis . . . they couldn't have better exercise.'
Besides, 'it is a cheap way of seeing one's friends and
much pleasanter than set dinner parties', she added. 'I
have a cake, a plate of thin bread and butter, and tea all
set out on a table in Peterhouse Garden, and Kate in her
pretty cap and apron to wait on everybody.' No one
minded that Mrs Jebb while she was on the courts wore
a little black velvet bag over her nose tied on with a
piece of elastic to keep the sun from damaging her complexion. She was a great beauty, with auburn hair and
'a charming Rubenesque countenance' and could command admiration for anything she chose to do.

Her tennis parties were the highlight of Cambridge
society in the eighties and the nineties and were also a
fruitful seed-bed for the pleasure she enjoyed more than
any other—matchmaking. Young men found her world-
liness alluring and came to her for advice, which she
gave freely with an invigorating sympathy. And they
were charming young men—the five sons of Charles
Darwin, the Balfour brothers and Tennyson's two boys;
young men who were modest about their intellectual
achievements, attractive and brilliant, without being
involved either in the aesthetic fads and fancies of their
time or with the tub-thumping, jingoistic heroes of the

Empire, so eager to adopt the white man's burden in Queen Victoria's dominions beyond the seas. Gerald Balfour, Mrs Jebb thought, was 'the most superior man I ever met', with an income of £1,000 a year 'and can call cousins with half the nobility of England.' She hoped he would be interested in her eldest niece from Philadelphia, but Nellie, even fitted out in her aunt's blue plush jacket done over from the year before, failed to respond; it was 'as hard to love up as to love down' apparently and as Gerald was 'full of earnest thoughts, working hard on philosophy and discoursing on Hegel', it is not surprising if Nellie found him quite beyond her.

Nellie was a disappointment; she refused George Darwin when he proposed and returned to Philadelphia unmatched in spite of all the opportunities her aunt had given her. But her sister Maud was a more promising pupil. She found Cambridge society 'the Utopia of all my fondest dreams' and her Aunt Cara a shrewd guide and mentor. 'It is wonderful to me the way she makes people admire her,' she wrote home to her mother in a letter full of excitement, describing the tennis parties and the tea parties and all the young men who were invited to the house. Gerald Balfour was 'just what you would imagine an English Lord to look and be like . . . he is so beautiful.' But Englishmen were 'strange creatures' and she did not find it easy to understand them. 'They all seem so simple and no boasting in their talk or manners. . . . Aunt C. says it is because they have their position in life generally and are not obliged to talk and act to keep it. When I think of these men and compare them with the class of gentlemen that are in society in West Philadelphia, I weaken. . . . The ones we should call ordinary, they call handsome and those we think handsome, they call ordinary.' It was all very puzzling and very exciting. And there was George Darwin 'coming in to see Aunt C. every day and sometimes twice a day. . . .

He is full of fun, intensely nervous, cannot sit still a minute and talks differently from an American man.'

Maud liked him very much and he was Aunt Cara's favourite among the Darwins. She was determined that Maud should not repeat Nellie's mistake and spoil her chances, writing long letters of advice to her when she went off on a trip to Italy with Darwin as a member of the party. 'Until you *are* engaged,' she warned, 'do not go out with him at all without a chaperon. You can sit and talk to him in the hotel drawing-room, at his motion, of course. I think you should show a tendency to withdraw from behaving to him as if he were a cousin, since he isn't. You know even in Philadelphia you would use judgement in giving a man your society, and you would take care not to be seen so much with him as to make people talk. In Florence you must be very particular. Besides, a man thinks none the worse of a girl for being a little particular. I have told George that your going with him so freely at Castellamare was exceptional, you had got to know him so well in Cambridge, that in his case you felt you might allow yourself to enjoy the benefit of his companionship without the fear that he would misunderstand you. Still it is now high time to make a change, and besides, all is very well that ends well. In Florence you are in the world again and will want to make a good impression. . . .' So the elegant handwriting went on sweeping across the page and the advice from the married woman was poured into the ear of the young maiden; though Mrs Jebb, without a qualm of conscience, calmly disowned her pleasure in pulling all the strings behind the scenes when she declared to George: 'Your family might think this was a match of my making. And it wasn't *one* bit, mind that. . . . If there is a suspicion I utterly and entirely repudiate, it is that of being a match-maker.'

George Darwin was thirty-eight and Maud only

twenty-two. But it was a happy marriage. They settled down in Cambridge with their four children and Maud took as much pleasure as her aunt in the gentle art of matchmaking. Her small daughter Gwen remembered being frequently 'sent along to play gooseberry in the boat or on some sightseeing expedition' with the courting couples who came in and out of the Darwins' rambling house, and her mother apparently never failed to see that all the conventions were observed. Yet she once wrote: 'It seems unutterably vulgar to me that girls who are well brought up, and sons who are well brought up, should not be allowed to associate without every girl having her mother at her elbow to see that no indecency is committed. The real truth is that the chaperons want the power in their own hands, and I believe, though they protest against it, they really enjoy the dances. . . . I hope that when Gwen grows up, there will be a revolution in this respect,' she added, 'and I hope that she will help to bring it around.'

Gwen did help—she was allowed 'to stop trying to be a young lady' and to go to the Slade School of Art when she grew up. And Maud Darwin lived to see her revolution come about, dying in 1947 at the age of eighty-six, by which time all restrictions on the leisure and pleasures of the young had vanished and it was no longer necessary for boys and girls to say where they were going or what they were doing to amuse themselves and each other. Even in the nineties the mothers and aunts and maiden ladies acting the duenna found it difficult to keep pace with the safety bicycle, which carried their charges out into the country and along the lanes in mixed parties or in tandem seclusion. Everyone took to cycling. The well-to-do from Belgravia, attended by a coachman and a footman, had their bicycles brought by carriage to Battersea Park and went for a spin before returning home by carriage. Katie Lawrence sang on the halls 'Daisy,

Daisy, give me your answer do!' and jokes about Mrs Bloomer's 'rational costume' abounded, though most of the ladies wore skirts that were called short because they came to their ankles. 'The wheel women of today and tomorrow,' the *Queen* noted in its editorial column, 'are sharp, wide-awake, aggressive, self-assertive. They know no fear, and what sense of shame they have wears a different aspect from their ancestors'. They stand no nonsense and need no help, save in matters appertaining to their machines.'

But it was useless for the editor of the *Queen* or Mrs Grundy and the puritans to go crying after them. The modern young woman of the nineties was riding her bicycle into the freedom of the twentieth century and nothing could stop her. She saw no reason why life should not become better and better. She had no idea that her leisure might one day be a thing of the past or that she might have to find her pleasure in doing the work her servants had always done for her.

Society was changing rapidly. The long conflict between religion and science had undermined the mental and moral convictions of the mid-Victorians. The emphatic principles of duty, self-sacrifice and discipline were no longer paramount. A return to the idleness, luxury and pleasure of the Regency was to be found among the opulent upper classes, and the prudish inhibitions of the middle classes no longer had the same strength to hinder their enjoyment of life. The young looked forward to greater independence from the family hearth; women no longer felt it was their duty to bear twelve or thirteen children; husbands found their authority diminishing. And when the widowed Queen finally sickened and died at Osborne in 1901, the moral power of the nation at last slipped from her small, plump hands. The nineteenth century was over—the problems of leisure and pleasure in the twentieth still to come.

SELECT BIBLIOGRAPHY

ALDBURGHAM, Alison. *Shops and Shopping.* 1964.
AUSTEN, Jane. *Letters.* Ed. R. W. Chapman. 1932.
BATTISCOMBE, Georgina. *Charlotte M. Yonge.* 1943
BATTISCOMBE, Georgina. *Mrs. Gladstone: Portrait of a Marriage*, 1956.
BEERBOHM, Max. *Works.* 1896.
BEERBOHM, Max. *More.* 1899.
BEERBOHM, Max. *Mainly on the Air.* 1946.
BLANCH, Lesley. *The Wilder Shores of Love.* 1954.
BOBBITT, Mary Reed. *With Dearest Love to All: The Life and Letters of Lady Jebb.* 1960.
BOLITHO, Hector. *Albert, Prince Consort.* 1964.
BOVILL, E. W. *The England of Nimrod and Surtees, 1815–54.* 1959.
BOVILL, E. W. *English Country Life, 1780–1830.* 1962.
BRITTAIN, Vera. *The Women at Oxford.* 1960.
BRONTË, Charlotte. *Letters.* Ed. Muriel Spark. 1954.
BYRON, Lord. *A Self Portrait in His Letters and Diaries.* Ed. Peter Quennell. 2 vols. 1950.
CARLYLE, Jane Welsh. *A New Selection of Her Letters.* Ed. Trudy Bliss. 1950.
CARLYLE, Thomas. *Letters to His Wife.* Ed. Trudy Bliss. 1953.
CARROLL, Lewis. *Diaries.* Ed. Roger Lancelyn Green. 2 vols. 1953.

CECIL, Lord David. *Melbourne*. 1965.

CHANCELLOR, E. Beresford. *Life in Regency and Early Victorian Times*. 1926.

CLARK, J. Kitson. *The Makings of Victorian England*. 1962.

CONNELY, Willard. *Count D'Orsay*. 1952.

CONSTABLE, John. *Correspondence*. Ed. R. B. Beckett. 2 vols. 1964.

COURTNEY, Janet. *Recollected in Tranquillity*. 1920.

CREEVEY. *The Creevey Papers*. Ed. Sir Herbert Maxwell. 1906.

DICKENS, Charles. *Letters*. Ed. House and Storey. 1965.

DISHER, M. Willson. *The Greatest Show on Earth*. 1937.

DUNBAR, Janet. *Mrs. G.B.S.* 1963.

EDEN, The Hon. Emily. *Letters*. Ed. Violet Dickinson. 1919.

EGAN, Pierce. *Life in London*. 1821.

ELIOT, George. *Letters*. Ed. R. Brimley Johnson. 1926.

FINCH, Edith. *Wilfrid Scawen Blunt*. 1938.

GAUNT, William. *The Aesthetic Adventure*. 1945.

GIBBS-SMITH, C. H. *The Great Exhibition of 1851*. 1950.

GREEN, Roger Lancelyn. *Authors and Places*. 1963.

GREVILLE, Charles. *Memoirs, 1821–65*. Ed. Roger Fulford. 1963.

GRONOW, Captain. *Reminiscences and Recollections*. Ed. John Raymond. 1964

HADDON, Archibald. *The Story of the Music Hall*. 1935.

HANSON, Lawrence and Elisabeth. *Marian Evans and George Eliot*. 1952.

HAYDON, Benjamin Robert. *Diaries*. Ed. Willard Bissell Pope. 5 vols. 1960.

HAYTER, Alethea. *Elizabeth Barrett Browning*. 1962.

HAZLITT, William. *Essays*. 1825.

HODGE, Edmund. *Enjoying the Lakes*. 1957.

HOLME, Thea. *The Carlyles at Home*. 1965.

HUNT, Leigh. *Autobiography*. 2 vols. 1903.

JACKSON, Holbrook. *The Eighteen Nineties*. 1922.

KEATS, John. *Letters*. Ed. Buxton Forman. 1948.
KEMBLE, Fanny. *Records of a Later Life*. 1882.
KILVERT, Francis. *Diary*. Ed. William Plomer. 1944.
LAMB, Charles. *Letters*. Ed. George Woodcock. 1950.
LAVER, James. *The Age of Optimism: Manners and Morals, 1849–1914*. 1966.
LAVER, James. *Whistler*. 1930.
LESLIE, Shane. *George IV*. 1926.
LIEVEN, Princess Dorothea. *Letters 1812–1834*. Ed. L. G. Robinson. 1902.
LOCHHEAD, Marion. *The Victorian Household*. 1964.
LUBBOCK, Percy. *Elizabeth Barrett Browning in Her Letters*. 1906.
LUTYENS, Mary. *Millais and the Ruskins*. 1967.
MANNING–SANDERS, Ruth. *Seaside England*. 1951.
MARSHALL, Mary Paley. *What I Remember*. 1947.
MAUROIS, André. *Disraeli*. 1927. Trans. Hamish Miles.
MAUROIS, Simone André. *Miss Howard and the Emperor*. 1957. Trans. Humphrey Hare.
McKENZIE, K. A. *Edith Simcox and George Eliot*. 1961.
MELVILLE, Lewis. *The Beaux of the Regency*. 2 vols. 1908.
MOERS, Ellen. *The Dandy*. 1960.
MORTIMER, Raymond, *The Jockey Club*. 1958.
MORTON, Frederic. *The Rothschilds, A Family Portrait*. 1962.
MUGGERIDGE, Kitty, and ADAM, Ruth. *Beatrice Webb: A Life*. 1967.
OLIVIER, Edith. *Four Ladies of Wiltshire*. 1945.
PALMERSTON, Lady. *Letters*. Ed. Tresham Lever. 1957.
PEEL, Mrs C. S. *The Stream of Time*. 1931.
PIMLOTT, J. A. R. *The Englishman's Holiday*. 1947.
POPE-HENNESSEY, James. *Monckton Milnes*. 2 vols. 1951.
POPE-HENNESSEY, Una. *Charles Dickens*. 1945.
PÜCKLER-MUSKAU, Prince Hermann. *A Regency Visitor*. Ed. E. M. Butler. 1957.
RAVERAT, Gwen. *Period Piece*. 1952.

RAY, Gordon Norton. *Life of Thackeray.* 2 vols. 1955.

ROLT, L. T. C. *Isambard Kingdom Brunel.* 1957.

ROWELL, George. *The Victorian Theatre: A Survey.* 1956.

SADLEIR, Michael. *Blessington-D'Orsay, A Masquerade.* 1933.

SALA, George Augustus. *Twice Round the Clock.* 1859.

SITWELL, Osbert, and BARTON, Mary. *Brighton.* 1935.

STIRLING, Monica. *The Fine and the Wicked: The Life and Times of 'Ouida'.* 1957.

STRACHEY, Lytton. *Queen Victoria.* 1921.

SYMONS, Arthur. *Aubrey Beardsley.* 1898.

TERRY, Ellen. *Memoirs.* 1933.

TERRY, Ellen, and SHAW, George Bernard. *A Correspondence.* Ed. Christopher St John. 1949.

TREVELYAN, George Macaulay. *English Social History.* Vol. 4. 1949.

VICTORIA, Queen. *Leaves from the Journal of Our Life in the Highlands.* Ed. A. Helps. 1868.

VICTORIA, Queen. *Letters.* Ed. Buckle. 3 vols. 1908.

WALBANK, F. A. *Queens of the Circulating Library.* 1950.

WATT, Margaret, H. *The History of the Parson's Wife.* 1943.

WELLINGTON, Duke of. *Letters.* Ed. 7th Duke of Wellington. 1965.

WHEATLEY, Vera. *The Life and Work of Harriet Martineau.* 1957.

WHITE, R. J. *Life in Regency England.* 1963.

WILDE, Oscar. *Letters.* Ed. Rupert Hart-Davis. 1962.

WILSON, Harriette. *Memoirs.* 1825.

WOODHAM-SMITH, Cecil. *Florence Nightingale.* 1950.

YOUNG, G. M. (Editor) *Early Victorian England.* 1934.

INDEX

© Cassell and Co. Ltd. 1969